D0212918

THE COMING REVOLUTION IN EDUCATION

Basic Education and the New Theory of Schooling

EUGENE MAXWELL BOYCE
Professor of Educational Administration
Bureau of Educational Studies and Field Services
College of Education
University of Georgia

UNIVERSITY
PRESS OF
AMERICA

LANHAM • NEW YORK • LONDON

Randall Library UNC-W

Copyright © 1983

by Eugene Maxwell Boyce

University Press of America,™ Inc.

4720 Boston Way
Lanham, MD 20706

3 Henrietta Street
London WC2E 8LU England

All rights reserved
Printed in the United States of America

ISBN (Perfect): 0-8191-3407-4
ISBN   (Cloth): 0-8191-3406-6

Contents

LC1035
.B69
1983

249092

Preface

The conditions are ripe for revolution in education except for one essential element: there has been no intellectual analysis, based on theory, of the mass of neutral results of research concerning student achievement. The required analysis has not been made because no sound theory has been advanced. The writer proposes such a theory. The theory is not only consistent with research findings; it permits new interpretation of the massive data, and gives direction to major reform. The level of frustration required for revolution is certainly present. Surely education cannot long persist in its old ways in the face of great and fundamental change.

In Chapter 1 (It Happened in Africa) I attempt to show, by citing personal experience, the critical nature of the need to develop a successful plan for universal education in free and democratic societies. Educational leaders in developing countries understand that promising universal education to the citizenry is a political necessity. They also know that universal education, in completely controlled societies, fits neatly into the system of complete control of the job market; they also know that in America we are still struggling to fit universal education into our social system. This is a critical point in maintaining democratic governments in developing countries. The failure of the United States to produce a viable system of universal education could well be the key factor that switches the developing world to communism.

In Chapter 2 (The End of an Age) I trace the great frustration concerning education to the Sputnik event of 1957, and show that education's response to the resulting public and political pressure has resulted in an education system characterized by "patch-work." This "patch-work" is largely the result of seeing specialization as the answer to all problems. Massive research in the last 25 years has failed to support the methods that have been introduced to improve education. I have suggested that the key to improvement in student achievement is the student's motivation; and that motivation to learn is a social phenomenon. This point of view has not been identified in the results of research because factors that correlate with learning have been classified as being "outside the school." The proposed new theory permits new interpretation of the data so that the data makes sense, and reveals its basic social nature.

In Chapter 3 (The New Theory of Schooling) I describe the new theory as having two dimensions based on two perceived motivational systems: One: The school assumes that it serves a monolithic society, and that the student is motivated by the value system of this closed society. Two: the school assumes that the student comes to school wanting what the school has to offer. If neither of these two assumptions can be made (they cannot be made if the students are from a polycultural society and if all children and youth of school age are in school), we are left with the assumption that motivation to learn what the school teaches must be generated at the school. Theory, in the first instance, is a description of the thing being theorized about. If we describe the school in terms of organization, teaching method, or curriculum; we seek improvement or understanding in organization, teaching method, and curriculum. If we describe the school in terms of the source of the student's motivation; we seek improvement on understanding in terms of the source of the student's motivation.

In Chapter 4 (Research Results and the New Theory) I

point out that the results of research since Sputnik (1957) have been largely neutral, and that these neutral results are the natural consequence of the lack of a viable theory. Other evidence of the lack of theory are (1) the preponderance of hierarchical schemes of development and (2) a total absence of any central thrust among the expert writers in education.

In Chapter 5 (An Overview of the New School) I give a limited description of the four centers that make up the school: (1) a medical center which in effect is a clinic and hospital for children and youth, (2) a school base, where the students live and work from during the school day. (3) A dramatic arts center which includes provision for instruction in musical arts, physical arts, and fine arts. And (4) a basic literacy center where teachers, by means of direct instruction, attempt to make the students literate in English, history, geography, mathematics, biology, and physical science.

In Chapter 6 (School Practice that Inhibits the Effectiveness of the New Theory) I show that certain highly valued school activities cannot be supported under the new theory, because they tend to polarize the student body into groups that have their bases outside the school. The most popular of these practices are: (1) the elective system, (2) vocational education, (3) grouping by ability and achievement, (4) interscholastic athletics, (5) grouping of students based on sex, (6) the gang toilet, and (7) the school lunchroom.

In Chapter 7 (The New Theory and the New Curriculum) I state that the curriculum is in two parts: (1) curriculum designed to build the classroom units into working groups. This is done by group activity in musical arts, physical arts, and fine arts. These three areas are combined periodically into a dramatic arts production for parents and the public. (2) Curriculum designed to make the students literate in a broad spectrum of knowledge. The students in formal classes will be instructed in the "languages of" English, history, geography, mathematics, biology and physical science.

In Chapter 8 (The New Theory Calls for New Teaching

Methods) I attempt to show why the long-term purpose of the school must be clearly stated, easily communicated, and free of ambiguity. It must be some essential ingredient of the social structure that can be contained within the bounds (territory) of the school, which can be participated in by all students, and does not force the individuals of the multi-cultural group to defend themselves in terms of their own identity based on outside-the-school groups. There must be a within-the-school culture that does not project itself to the outside community. I propose that this central long-term goal for the pre-adult student is: to achieve that level of literacy that is necessary to a full life in a technical society that has a scientific base. I have described all literacy instruction as in the "language mode." I show that the support for this "mode" is based in cognitive psychology. A learning theory that supports the proposed method of instruction is generated by adding the search finding concerning the short-term memory to the research findings in cognitive psychology. From the same sources I make a case for writing as the basic literacy component. Multi-cultural literacy development depends on the school's ability to build a classroom unit into a working group. This group must be maintained by direct, whole-group instruction.

In Chapter 9 (Summary) I summarize the logic of the theory. This chapter is not a summary of the whole book because the book itself is a summary statement of the theory.

In Chapter 10 (A Final Word) I suggest that education in America is too involved in the economic and political structure to solve its problems by slow evolution, and that fundamental change cannot take place just because someone has a good idea. The magnitude of the change needed in public education requires that it must await some major social or political crisis. I have two purposes in writing this book: to help educators better understand their frustrations in trying to do what seems to be an impossible job, and to put the theory into the public record for future use in time of crisis. I am unable to predict the crisis that will make the new school possible. I do, however, identify two sure trends that will lead to the necessary conditions: the move toward a federal medical program for children and youth, and the rush of women into the job market. I again warn the reader that the theory fits only a specific situation: where the school assumes that it serves a poly-cultural society, and where all children and youth of school age are presumed to belong in school.

1   Introduction

It Happened in Africa

"Oh My God," I said, with my head in my hands. It just popped out, I didn't mean for anyone to hear. A man next to me at the table said, "What did you say? Are you in pain?"

It's a meeting in Africa in 1970. Around the table are the chief professional education officers of the twelve states of Nigeria and the deans of education of the four universities. It's the Nigeria Educational Research Council and I am the American advisor.

"Are you in pain?" —I was in pain, but it was from a painful thought. —To myself I was reviewing my own professional history: principal of a small rural school, superintendent of a small district school system, principal of a large secondary school, director of a laboratory school in a large university, associate dean of a college of education in a large university, USAID advisor to the Ministry of Education in Ethiopia, director of a federally funded research and development center with an annual budget of $800,000, advisor to the Nigeria Educational Research Council. I felt as if I had been in as many education planning sessions, in as many different places, under as many different economic, social, and political conditions as any man alive.

The painful thought: *Educational planners say the same things over and over, no matter what the conditions, no matter where they are; educators say the same things, just as if those things had never*

1

been said before." And this painful thought merged into another (I don't know which came first, they seemed to come at the same time). "Around this table are the top education people of Nigeria. We are charged with building a public school system for all children and youth that will help to unify the country after a period of intense civil war. . . . *Not a person in this room will send his children to these schools we are planning for 'the people.'*" Are the two ideas related? Why should they come at the same time? And why should they depress me so?

Universal education through secondary school is a government promise in all developing countries. It is a *political necessity*. This is clearly understood by education officials in developing countries. The political nature of this promise is not clearly understood by educators in America, probably because it came so slowly, over a 200 year period.

I was education advisor to the Ministry of Education of Ethiopia before their revolution, and advisor to the Nigeria Educational Research Council after their civil war. Poverty reigned in Ethiopia, but the Emperor preached that education is the answer to poverty. Hope was high in Nigeria (Never a poor country, and now the prospect of a large national income from oil). The two countries are as different as two countries can be, but they have a common concern for universal education. Educators in developing countries know that the promise of universal public education as government policy is a *political necessity*. They also know that the presence of large numbers of educated people without jobs almost certainly guarantees political revolution. I was as certain in 1968 that a revolution was pending in Ethiopia as if I had had divine inspiration.

There was a story in Ethiopia that the spring graduates of the Haile Selassie University would, in the fall, gather as a group on the steps of the Imperial Palace and await an audience with the Emperor. When the Emperor appeared, a spokesman for the group would say, "Your Imperial Highness, at your request we have become educated in your university. Now we need jobs, so we can use our education to serve our country." It is said that the Emperor would allocate the young men to the several government ministries, and tell the ministries to give them jobs. When such a process is necessary, we have the sure seeds of revolution.

Nigeria is relatively rich, but they have the same basic problem in public education. In Lagos I was asked to take part in a meeting at the USAID director's office at which they would determine the fate of the U.S. sponsored comprehensive secondary school at Port Harcourt. The serious students had fled the school leaving only the unmotivated. The Nigerians in charge of the school recommended that the comprehensive program be abolished; the American education advisor responsible for the school made the same recommendation. After a long discussion in which we all took part, the USAID director said, "I appreciate your advice, but we will continue the comprehensive program at Port Harcourt because it is U.S. government policy."

Why does the Nigerian Educational Research Council have an *American* advisor? Nigeria is not poor, but there is always a struggle for political power. Developing countries see the political issues as polarized around two concepts of government. "Democratic" is usually associated with the U.S., and "communist" or "socialist" with the USSR. Both systems sponsor universal education as a device to gain the support of the people. If the "in" government is democratic, it will usually have American education advisors. The education officials are usually highly educated and do not need "advice." They usually already know anything the American can tell them. The American is a part of the symbolic system that is visible evidence that the government is doing all it can to move toward a universal education system appropriate to the ideals of the government in power. The leadership is thoroughly familiar with the education system in America and quite conscious of the difficulties we have and the growing discontent in the U.S. concerning education. They also know that they have no choice but to support the system. Non-support would furnish political fuel to the opposition.

In the communist ideology the function of universal education is clear, and easily understood. Universal education fits neatly into the authoritarian state. Education is tied directly to jobs—control of the job being the critical control point in an authoritarian state. Level of education, and consequently the level of employment, is determined first, by level of achievement in school. They do not educate people for jobs that do not exist. No such direct, controlled, relationship between education and jobs exists in democratic countries.

It should be clear that the success, or plans for education that project success, is a critical factor in a country that could swing from democratic to communist in a single election or coup. The government of a developing country that claims to be democratic does not dare admit that it has no clearly workable plan for universal education in a democracy. So we see the function of the American advisor.

Then why do we say the same things over and over in education meetings? We say the same things because we do not yet have a viable plan for universal education in a democratic society. The things we repeat over and over are the symbolic, ritualistic words and phrases that belong to an economic, social, and political environment that no longer exists. Jerome Bruner's "clever maxims and moralistic resolutions" are identified as the ritualistic symbolism that declares that we are members of a cult that has no viable theory to apply to the changed conditions in which we find ourselves. This education talk is remarkably similar to scientific discussions before the scientific breakthrough of Galileo and Newton just before and after 1600. Organizations and institutions always turn to ritualism based on symbols when the institution continues after the need is gone or when the system turns and feeds on itself instead of moving forward. So: *"Oh, My God, we say the same things in Nigeria, in Ethiopia, and in America!"* And why does the Nigerian educator see something the American educator does not see? Because of the time factor. The United States grew into a system of universal education through the secondary school level during a time period of 200 years. The Nigerian, from political necessity, is forcing into a very few years the change from very limited enrollment in colonial or missionary schools to a system of universal education. They need to see the system begin to work effectively in a five-year plan, or at most a ten-year plan. A single group of educators can witness and direct the whole process from beginning to maturity. But most of all, they see clearly that what they are doing is based on *political necessity*; They are not "do-gooders" operating from "moralistic resolutions."

The Nigerian educator can see the students flee from the comprehensive secondary school or the "modern" elementary school. The serious students will attend these schools only if there is no other choice. The students know that the key to success in a developing scientifically based technical society is not learning to use a screwdriver or a wrench. They know that the key is literacy in the language of commerce (the lingua franca). They know that the technical books are not written in Yoruba, Hausa, or Ibo. They know that people do not flee the farm because they do not know how to farm. They know that farming, if successful in Nigeria, will, as in the U.S., be as scientifically and technically based as is the petroleum refining center.

In America the educator does not see the students flee the school because the fleeing student never leaves the building. They do not see that the school is a better base for an organized gang than is the street. They do not seem to grasp the idea that the books that contain the knowledge necessary for active participation in the good life of the U.S. are not written in street language nor can they be. They do not see the economic, social, and cultural forces that preserve an established education system that has little to do with the learning process at school.

Why do I think I know something that other American educators do not? I went to Ethiopia in 1965 as USAID advisor to the ministry of education because a friend, in USAID Washington, who was responsible for the Ethiopian program, asked me to go for two years "to find out the trouble there."

(I found the trouble and reported it, but the bureaucratic structure prevented any solution.) I was free to learn more than the normal USAID advisor because: (1) I was regular hire (inside the structure, not contract) so I could read all the documents and sit in all the policy sessions as a regular government man. The only official who knew I was temporary was my employing friend. I was not interested in doing things for my own advancement in the organization. This freed me to work with the Ethiopians instead of the other Americans. This extended into informal social contacts as well as my official work. (2) I was 52 years old with unusually broad American educational experience. Educators with similar background were usually under contract to USAID for a specific job, and they did not have access to the official organizational structure as did the direct hire people. (3) I have a life-long interest in the history of theory development in the physical sciences. (4) I have a strong background in chemistry and physics. (5) I have a marked suspicion of dogma, even dogma in the scientific areas. (6) I knew, or I quickly learned, that I was not taking knowledge to an uneducated or ignorant educational leadership.

My job in Nigeria was unique. I was paid in an indirect manner by the U.S. government, but I was to act as if I were hired by the Nigerian Ministry of Education. I was hired by the Overseas Liaison Committee of the American Council on Education, and paid through the African-American Institute. When the hiring agency contacted me, they gave as a reason, my "reputation for being able to work with the local people in a foreign environment."

I met the executive secretary of the Nigeria Educational Research Council, J. M. Akintola, at my initial meeting with the Minister of Education. Akintola's (it's good form to call him "Akintola") first remark to me was (almost in anger), "Why don't you stay in the United States and solve your own educational problems before you try to help us in Africa?" It was a better question than he knew. I knew, but he didn't know that I knew, that I had learned in Ethiopia that I was not to bring the word from America to a backward nation (Akintola had two advanced degrees from England after six years of study there). I did not then tell Akintola why I had come to Nigeria.

When I was contacted about the job, I was finishing two years as director of the Research and Development Center in Educational Stimulation (actually one and one-half years as director and six months as program director). The federal government closed the operation at that time after five years and four million dollars. The center was dedicated to early learning (beginning with two-and-a-half and three-year-olds) and sequential curriculum as the solution to the education of the disadvantaged. We didn't gain the slightest clue concerning the solution to that educational problem. Two other centers thought they did. At least they sold the feds on the idea that the solution lay in a micro-sequenced curriculum with an individualized program for each child. I was beginning to suspect that the solution had to do more with social and cultural factors; probably from reflection on my Ethiopian experience. The opportunity to go to Nigeria when their great civil war was scarcely over (the war officially ended on January 15, 1970; I arrived there on July 15 that same year) was an opportunity that I could not refuse. I had followed that war closely from press accounts, and I knew that internally Nigeria was as divided (three ways, not two) as any place in the world. I suspected that more could be learned at that time and in that place than at any time and place in the history of the world about building a public education system in a poly-cultural society. Furthermore, I believed that I was in a position, mentally and experientially, to learn it, if it were there to learn.

When I returned to the University of Georgia and to the program for the education of school administrators, my boss, Dr. Doyne Smith, (a very wise man) asked me, "What do you want to teach?" My immediate answer, "Theory." After about three class sessions teaching "theory" I was very uncomfortable, knowing that there was no theory. Struggling with this confusion of the mind, I realized that I had a theory. It forced its way into my consciousness without direct effort on my part. I think I have made an important discovery. Whether I can convey it through the printed page, the reader will have to decide.

Chapter 2

The End of an Age

Great Frustration in Educational Leadership. Education's response to the public cry for a "return to basic education" is a reflection of the great frustration felt by educational leadership confronted with enormous social change in America and in the whole world. Basic education is interpreted as "reading and numbers" because that is the way the people and the lawmakers have been saying it. There is a wide-spread instinctive understanding of the fact that nothing can take the place of functional literacy for those who are to benefit from living in a society based on scientific technology. Because the field of professional education is unable to provide the practicing educational leader with sound direction based on viable theory, educational leadership has turned to simple, crude response to pressure without serious analysis of what the "teach them to read and figure" really means. One system superintendent told the writer, "I'll tell you what I do. I call the parents together and ask them what to do. If it doesn't work, it's *their* fault." More sophisticated versions of this process have become high virtue in educational administration. Some versions are expressed in terms of "communication systems."

Sputnik Changed Everything. The American people's concern for the directional drift of public education, growing slowly for a long time, came into sharp focus in 1957 when the USSR placed Sputnik, the first space satellite, into orbit. For this event to have been interpreted as a fundamental weakness of the public schools seems rather odd. Perhaps, not so odd when we consider the faith Americans have in education as the foundation stone for the "good life," and the growing, unexpressed discontent with the top-heavy, government bureaucracy that has slipped control from parents and local leaders. So considered, the public demand for improvement looms as a long over-due explosion.

The Pattern of Education is a Colossal Patch-Work. In 1957 the developmental pattern of public education was well established. The takeover by the system superintendent was almost complete. The building principal, except for a few brave souls who continued to buck the system, had become middle management personnel. The Brown decision (school integration) of 1954 was sitting there waiting to blast the educational world. It was Sputnik (1957) that exposed the vulnerability of public education. It was the Brown decision that rushed into the open wound. Having no preparation for either Sputnik or Brown, and having little time, and leadership unprepared or unable to re-examine the purpose and function of public education in the face of dramatic change, education proceeded to build a patch-work system that would be comical if it were not so overpowering in its cancerous growth. The patches have taken over the whole garment, so that the foundation garment is hardly visible. Remedial procedures have become the mode.

Imagine the management of a shoe factory continuing to produce so many defective shoes that the major function of workers in the factory is to patch-up the shoes before the product is sent to market. Wouldn't good management examine the basic manufacturing process instead of simply adding more and more workers to expand the patching?

Attempts to Save the System. Years from now educational analysts will be amazed at the paradoxical efforts experts have used in attempts to "save" the system. It will be difficult to explain how adoption of management procedures, deemed so successful in the manufacturing and business world (and in getting us to the moon), have led to the present patch-up approach rather than to a basic re-examination of the whole system. There was a similar condition in medicine, with its humors, vapors, and solids just prior to the advent of germ theory. When there is no valid theory or when useful theory outlives the empirical evidence, the mind turns more and more to elaborate schemes and hierarchical arrangements, most of which carry the name of some authority in that field. Ptolemy in the publication of "The Almagest" made almost permanent the system of epicycles and deferents designed to save the geocentric system, keeping the earth at the center of the universe. From his powerful authority position, Aristotle helped preserve the four element system (fire, air, water, and earth) by "explaining" the elements in a two dimensional grid system in which the second dimension was hot, cold, wet, and dry. Even the modern scientific world will rally around an absurd "explanation" if that explanation will save a comfortable theory.

Even Scientists Try to Save Defunct Theory. At the turn of the century physical science was secure in the wave theory of light. Waves must have a medium through which to travel. If light is to travel by wave motion there needs to be such a medium between the earth and the other bodies in space. The American scientists attempted to establish the existence of the medium (called "ether") by showing the effect of the earth moving through the ether as the earth moves around the sun. With superb instrumentation and sound procedures, Michelson and Morley failed to establish the existence of the ether. Their "no ether" announcement left the wave theory of light in shambles. Lorentz and Fitzgerald, well-known and reputable scientists, saved the system by proposing that the instrument designed to measure the motion of the earth through the ether shortened and lengthened itself just enough to compensate for the earth's motion, making it impossible to detect the ether. They supported their position by producing a workable mathematical formula for predicting the changes in instrument length due to motion. This is a classic example of modern scientists' efforts to save poor theory.

Specialization as Salvation. A wealth of data has been produced in the last quarter century concerning attempts to improve education. Educators have produced a wealth of explanations designed to save the old system. It is a major thesis of this book that attempts to improve education have been based on unrecognized, unexpressed, but consistent theory. The search for this theory took its form and structure from the Max Weber bureaucratic (production) model which assumes that efficiency stems primarily from specialization. When the product is easily recognized and clearly defined, such as an automobile or a shoe, the limits of specialization are determined by the structure of the product. The automobile has wheels, and wheels can be manufactured as units and added to the product in units. When the product cannot be clearly described it is not easily subject to this type of analysis and synthesis. In education there is no clear direction for specialization and no inherent limits to the specialty development process. The result is a chain reaction. Once the process is begun there is a self-generation of power to continue the process. Each succeeding stage feeds on the previous one with no limiting factors to draw the process to an end. Every phase of schooling is generating its own specialties. The general area of counseling is divided into many areas, each requiring special training. There are curriculum specialists and specialists in each area of curriculum. There are specialists in instruction with many different specialties in teaching method. There are specialties based on the classification of students. Administration and supervision are developing their own specialties as well as the specialties in administration and supervision required by the other specialties in the organization. One thing is assumed to be certain; it all requires more and more specialized personnel. All might be justified if the results were translated into student achievement. The facts are to the contrary.

Research Has Exposed the Grand Delusion. Achievement data and the results of educational research based on extensive government schemes and projects designed to improve education echo a consistent theme; no significant difference between control groups and experimental groups; no measurable improvement from old to new. Such results should lead educators to examine seriously the assumptions (theories) upon which all this work is based. The primary instinct for self-preservation prevents the examination of the basic theory. The unrecognized basic theory which begs for examination assumes "that children learn because teachers teach." The idea that the primary factors influencing student achievement have their roots outside the school is hardly a viable option available to the professional educator. The writer argues that motivation to learn is a social, societal, or cultural phenomenon, and that this interpretation has been suppressed by the illusion that for many years in America all children of school age have been regularly attending school. This illusion was exposed by Sputnik (1954).

The Roots of Motivation. The mistaken notion that motivation to learn originates within the school probably came from the fact that each student brings his/her motivation to school, or that motivation had its roots in the monolithic society of which the student was a part. In the case of a few students, motivation is essentially the desire to gain admission to a cultural group through the process of formal education. The notion "that students learn because teachers teach" can hardly be maintained when large numbers of students, after many years of schooling, fail to learn to read and figure at an acceptable minimal level.

Educational Thought is Still in the Pre-Galileo-Newton Age. The writer will attempt to show that educators are as helpless in finding the way out of the present confusion and frustration as were pre-Galileo and pre-Newton scientists and philosophers in trying to understand the basic structure of the natural world. There is a striking parallel in the two situations.

The age of science was born when Galileo found that the velocity of a free-falling body is not determined by the weight of that body, as had been supposed since the time of Aristotle some nineteen hundred years before. To understand that this discovery should have led directly to the scientific revolution requires some technical knowledge of the concept of cause and effect before and after this historic event. Prior to the Galileo-Newton era, cause and effect consisted of subject and predicate, the actor and the thing acted upon. The thing acted upon could be an inanimate object, but the actor (the cause) was always given anthropomorphic characteristics. The new concept of cause and effect, introduced by Galileo and generalized by Newton was totally revolutionary. It abandoned the anthropomorphic cause and identified every action as having two components with no inherent clue as to which component is actor (originating the action) and which is the object (acted upon). Newton called it "mutual action."

Motivation to Learn is a Social Phenomenon. The writer contends that attempts to improve education since Sputnik (1957) have been based on pre-Galileo-Newton models of cause and effect, and that attempts to apply models based on the modern scientific cause and effect have never been introduced. The writer will show that learning is an interaction process, similar to the basic laws of nature developed by Newton. This interaction process is called "social" when applied to human beings; and is summarized in the expression: *Motivation to learn is a social phenomenon*. It is proposed that educational leaders give attention to the school as a social institution. This means that the school should be so structured that motivation to learn what is taught by the school has its prime origin in the social structure of the school itself.

Group Learning is Disappearing from the Schools.
Histories of education are written with few references to theories of schooling. This leaves us with little basis for determining what has been valuable in the past, and few if any standards for determining what should be preserved and what should be allowed to die. So, the one-room school with one teacher was looked upon as a necessary evil to be done away with as soon as possible. If the one-room school is seen as producing a good learning situation, there is no basis for judging whether its strength was in the nature of the continuous group or in the continuous teacher. Next came the graded school in which the continuous group was preserved. Then came the departmentalized school still preserving the continuous group. Then the elective system, which was considered quite superior. If the elective system had real virtue or advantage it also had one great disadvantage; it began the destruction of the continuous group. Within the elective system it was still possible to use the power of the group process in the individual classroom provided the teacher recognized its value and understood how to use it. With the advent of individualized instruction, and individualized plans for each child, the force of the social process in learning was almost completely eliminated. This does not argue that there have been no advantages in the development of the great, complex, bureaucratic structures called schools. It does argue that for each advantage there has been a significant loss, because the importance of motivation to learn as a social phenomenon involving the group has not been recognized.

Motivational Factors are Outside the School. How will the educational world respond as the neutral results of research, experimentation, and major government programs, become more generally recognized? The neutral nature of the results has been intolerable, almost insulting, to educational leaders and policymakers. The first and most general response was attempts to refute the findings by publishing refutations in journals and books. This approach is still being exploited.

Some leading writers have accepted the strong evidence that the major factors influencing student achievement are outside the school, and as such are not subject to school control. Some leaders who recognize that these outside factors are social in nature, are urging that the social context be introduced into the education process by placing students outside the school, or by bringing the outside into the school building.

Effects of the Piece-Meal Growth of Public Education. Those responsible for organized education in America find it hard to admit that the present scheme of education with its many streams based on student ability, its universal preference for "practical" programs and job training, was actually developed from the piece-meal response to the gradual influx of students who have no motivation to accept traditional schooling. Educational leadership prefers the illusion that the present system of education is the result of sound planning and sound theory. Hardly anyone ever asked, "Where is the best place to train a person for a job?" The answer would bring to the surface our most pressing and unsolved problem: How do we deal with unemployment in a technical society that needs fewer and fewer man-hours of work? Organized education has often become the buffer zone to absorb the unemployed in a socially acceptable manner. Training a person for a job creates no job except for the teacher and the organization that provides the training. The reason we do not take the student out of school and put him/her on the job is because one of the school's unannounced functions is to keep people off the job market. If job training is coupled with eventual employment of the student in the establishment that trains him/her, it becomes quite apparent that too many are trained for the few jobs that exist.

The End-product of Social and Political pressure. The Brown decision and the civil rights movement put the cap on a social and political decision that had been developing for many years. That decision is summed up in the statement: *All* *pre-adults belong in school.* A universal human characteristic is the ability to produce rational and highly moralistic reasons for doing what we must do, and educators are no exception in this self-deception. The normal response of educators to the political decision to put all pre-adults in school (and to keep them there) is their conclusion that formal education for the pre-adult is the solution to all problems; social, political, and personal.

There is a Viable Alternative. The writer proposes that there is a viable alternative to the general conclusion that the major factors that influence student achievement are outside the school. An equally valid interpretation is that motivation to learn is a social phenomenon *whether in school or out.* The primary forces that influence student achievement are, in fact, now largely outside the school, but they need not be. The structure of the studies which conclude that the primary forces are outside the school are such that the influence of social and cultural forces on learning is not clearly identified. The interpretation of this data has emphasized the physical location of the forces (outside the school) rather than its general nature (social and cultural). The operation of these forces inside the school has hardly been studied at all. That the school can be a *primary* source of social forces designed to influence learning has not been suggested until now.

The New Theory Provides a New Interpretation of the Data. That the school can be a dominant source of social forces to influence student achievement is the primary thrust of this book. A new theory is required which first provides the basis for a new interpretation of the massive data that now exists; and second; requires a theory that provides direction for educational development based on the new interpretation. The strength and the weakness of the proposed theory is that the new program cannot be an add-on program to what we now have. It requires a complete restructuring of the school based on the new theory. The new theory gives no support to the development of larger and larger schools. It gives no support to the many streams and the continuous addition of new specialties whose ultimate goal is a different and personal program for each student. The new school will have a single short-term purpose: to provide, in a society in which all adults are expected to work, a wholesome, healthy, disciplined place for children and youth. The new school will have a single long-term purpose: to produce maximum literacy in the pre-adult population. Maximum literacy means: extension of literacy both vertically and horizontally. Vertically means the extension of literacy to as high a level as possible. Horizontally means literacy in as many areas as possible. A literacy area is defined as a dimension of knowledge that has its own basic language. It is the educator's responsibility to produce a school in which the two functions support and reinforce each other.

A Preview of What is to Follow. The rest of the book is devoted to the statement of the new theory of schooling; showing how the new theory makes sense of the findings of research; how the new theory projects a new concept of schooling; and how the new theory leads to a new organization, new teaching methods, and a new curriculum.

Chapter 3

The New Theory of Schooling

The New Theory Has Two Dimensions. In its most basic form, theory is a description of the thing being theorized about; in this case the school. The new theory is based on the assumption that motivation to learn is essentially a social/societal/cultural phenomenon (the logic for this assumption is established later). The new theory is a two dimensional model which divides motivation into (1) group and (2) individual components, each depends on social reinforcement for its power. These two components describe two basic types of schools.

The First Dimension. A TYPE ONE SCHOOL, is a school in which it is assumed that the student's motivation to learn what the school teaches is provided by a monolithic social group of which the student is a part. It is presumed that a monolithic society is a closed society and that an education system produced by such a group would reflect the most fundamental values of the group. It is presumed that the student would be surrounded by an environment of continual reinforcement for what the school teaches. Such a system of instruction and reinforcement would produce maximum achievement for the group.*

*This TYPE ONE SCHOOL was called "Village-Tribal" in the original theory paper (Boyce 1976), based on three years if educational work in the min-

19

The Second Dimension. A TYPE TWO SCHOOL is a school in which it is assumed that the student attends the school because he/she wants something the school has to offer. This "something" may or may not be the expressed purpose of the school. In any case, the motivation to learn is an attribute of the individual student. It is assumed that the students select themselves, based on the students' perception of what is to be gained by school attendance. Such a school would by definition be "not-for-everybody." The students' motivation is primarily social in that the student attends school because he/she wishes to improve status or level in the present social group, or because there is a desire to move into another social group through the medium of education.*

The Test of a Theory: Usefulness. The reader should not fall into the trap of concluding that it is here proposed that there exists, or has existed, in the United States TYPE ONE or TYPE TWO schools. Whether such schools exist or have existed is beside the point. The test of the theory is whether analysis, based on the theory, has a high probability of leading to school improvement.

Where the Theory Fits. A second caution is proposed at this point: the theory is designed to be useful in the American school where there is a presumed cultural mix and where all children are presumed to be in school. The theory is

istries of education in Ethiopia and Nigeria. "Village-Tribal" is the education system of the village; presumed to be a closed social system.
*The TYPE TWO SCHOOL was called "Missionary-Colonial" in the original theory paper (Boyce 1976). The political leadership in the developing countries of Africa use the promise of "education-for-all" to gain the popular support of the citizens. The writer was involved in the attempted rapid expansion of education in Ethiopia and Nigeria. He felt that there was a basic flaw in the system. The missionary school or the colonial school, by its very nature, is "not-for-everybody," and not expandable to "for-everybody" schools. Attempts at fundamental change from this established system produces a condition of non-support by the citizenry. So the "not-for-everybody" school was called "Missionary-Colonial." This may have been the beginning of the new theory.

not needed if those responsible for school policy perceive that they operate in either a TYPE ONE or a TYPE TWO situation.

Is There an Old Theory of Schooling? No! There is in fact a *system* of schooling now in general operation. When school people found themselves under great pressure to improve education following the Sputnik event(1957), efforts to improve schooling fell quickly into the production/factory model. It takes little imagination to see that the major education improvement projects of the last 25 years fit rather neatly into this structure. Dr. John I. Goodlad came to the same conclusion in his monumental work, "A Study of Schooling." He wrote: "The prevailing production model of schooling is powerful and seductive; it will be around for a long time to come. . . . Earlier, we expressed doubts about the utility of the factory/production model of schooling in seeking to describe or improve schools. . . . The production model has become less attractive to us than it was at the outset of this study (Goodlad 1979)." The new theory assumes that motivation to learn what the school teaches is a social phenomenon and that this motivation as represented in TYPE ONE and TYPE TWO schools has its roots outside the school. If present schools are poly-cultural, they cannot be TYPE ONE; if all children are in school, the schools cannot be TYPE TWO. This forces policymakers to conclude that the motivation to learn (the means of production) is to be found within the school and under the control of the school organization. A basic assumption in the factory/production model is that the means of production are within the factory and under the control of the organization.

The New Theory Defines a Third Type of School. A TYPE THREE SCHOOL is one in which it is assumed that motivation to learn what the school teaches is generated within the school. This is consistent with the factory/production model. When we apply the assumption that underlies the new theory (that motivation to learn is a social phenomenon), we conclude that the means of motivation are centered in some kind of social or group process. The policymakers, faced with pressure to improve student achievement, in a poly-cultural setting, with all children in school, were correct in concluding that motivation to learn must be assumed to be within the school. They were incorrect in assuming that substantial change in student achievement could be accomplished by the manipulation of school organization, teaching method, and curriculum, within the normal variation permitted within the existing system.

The Social Environment of the School is the Key. The theory leads to the almost inescapable conclusion that any significant improvement in student educational outcomes must come from motivation within the school and that this motivation must grow from the social environment of the school. This environment must be specifically described. It involves the building of strong student groups, direct teaching in groups involving extensive teacher-student interaction, and a single basic curriculum for all students.

"Social," in the New Theory Means "Interaction." The great discovery, by Galileo and Newton (Galileo died the year Newton was born: 1642) that ushered in the age of science, was that the laws of nature in their most basic form, are laws of interaction. It would not do violence to the new theory to suggest that the theory is a proposal that we look to the most fundamental laws of nature for direction in solving the problems of poly-cultural education. The following statements relate each of Newton's three laws of motion to the problem of teaching reading to children who identify themselves with a non-reading culture. Social, in this book, means interaction; taking its clue from Newton's three laws of motion.

Newton's first law: *Every body preserves its state of rest or of uniform motion in a right line, unless it is compelled to change that state by forces impressed thereon.* (Applied to a non-reading group this means that the state of non-reading is dynamic, not static. To teach reading to this group, we must overcome an active social force, not apathy.)

Newton's second law: *The acceleration produced by an unbalanced force is proportional to the unbalanced force and is inversely proportional to the inertia of the body.* (Applied to a non-reading group, this means that the social pressure is directly against the act of reading, not just the social results of not reading. If this is overcome, the pressure to overcome must be directed against the force that causes the non-reading: the social environment.)

Newton's third law: *To every action there is always opposed an equal reaction. The mutual actions of two bodies upon each other are always equal and oppositely directed.* (No force can act alone. For gravity to work two "somethings" must have mass. For an electrical force to work, two "somethings" must have an electrical charge. A "something" with mass only cannot attract or repel a "something" that has electrical charge only. A non-reading child cannot respond to reading instruction unless the child possesses some of the attributes that can respond to reading instruction. New attributes can be added only in a social or group environment. The only force available is the child's desire to be in or stay in a group).

The Meaning of "Social" for the Very Young Child. The primary interaction system for the very young is that interaction between the child and adults. The young child sees the adult as a source of meaning. The actions of the adult are associated with words. The words become generalized and disassociated from the specific actions of the adult. When this happens the child has moved from the affective to the cognitive domain. At this point the learning process becomes very rapid, with the child using every ruse he/she can devise to keep the attention of the adult. The source of knowledge and meaning is the adult; the means of acquisition is language (discussed later in the Methods chapter in relation to the work of Vygotsky and Luria and the beginning of cognitive psychology). While the primary interaction is between the child and the adult, the child delights in displaying this adult approval and the newfound knowledge before other children. So the maximum learning environment for the young child is language involvement with an adult while the child is part of an ongoing group.

The Meaning of "Social" for the Older Child. By the time the child is 12 or 13 years old we are in the center of what is popularly called "peer influence." Wise children of this chronological age who have a good thing at home (protection from the buffets of the outside world, money for the essential needs of life, parents who have influence in the dominant social system, automobiles for transportation, etc.) protect their family and parents from knowledge of the strength of the peer group's influence. Most children in this protected situation "go along" with the expectations of parents and kin through college, if financial support is available at home for that purpose.

If the home is not a part of the controlling level of our society, the controlling elements in the children's life are quite different. In this case, growing children must seek their social protection elsewhere, usually building groups or "gangs" that are considered antisocial by the controlling elements of the society.

In the American culture, for the majority of children and youth, the peer influence seems to reach a peak at approximately 12 or 13 years of age. Carvin Brown, in a study of Georgia school children found, that the effects of socioeconomic status (actually, in each school district; the percent of poverty, family income, education of adults, and percentage of free lunches) was almost nil at the 8th grade level. At the 4th grade level these four factors covered from 40% (for percent poverty) to 23% (percent free lunches) of the factors that are related to school achievement. The effect of these factors moved back upward to approximately 10% at the 11th grade level

(Brown, 1978). Dr. Brown in his study, did not relate this data to peer influence. The writer did, as a logical deduction of the new theory of schooling, suggest this relationship.

> Percentage figures represent the cumulative percent of vari-ance in district (school systems of Georgia) average achieve-ment test scores accounted for by the four socioeconomic variables listed. Academic achievement for 4th and 8th grades were measured by the Iowa Test of Basic Skills (ITBS) and for the 11th grade, the Tests of Academic Progress (TAP). The writer is suggesting that the peer influence is so strong in eighth grade that the strongest forces (SES factors) that retard student achievement hardly exist at that level (Boyce, 1978).

Of course the 8th graders of low SES are very much behind at this level. The study was designed to reflect the added influ-ence, not the accumulated influence of these factors.

The peer influence, as a factor in student academic achieve-ment, is very much related to the social setting of which the school is a part. Probably the best work in this area was done by Urie Bronfenbrenner and reported in his book: *Two Worlds of Childhood: U.S. and U.S.S.R.* Quoting Dr. Bronfenbrenner directly:

> Finally, there is evidence already cited from our own re-search that the peer group has quite different effects in the Soviet Union and in the United States. In the former, it operates to reinforce adult-approved patterns of conduct, whereas in our country, it intensifies antisocial tenden-cies. . . . In summary, the effect of a peer group on the child depends on the attitudes and activities which prevail in that peer group. Where group norms emphasize academic achievement the members perform accordingly; where the prevailing expectations call for violation of adult norms, these are as readily translated into action (Bronfenbrenner 1970, p. 108).

This rather long discussion of *The Meaning of "Social" for the Older Child* is to show the prevailing direction of the peer influence in the American society and to show that any reasonable attack on the problems of poly-cultural learning must deal with the social setting in which the learning is supposed to take place. For the older child we must recognize the importance of group-building. It follows that the school must make its primary concern the building of groups that are identified with the school and its territory. It is the proposal here that the best learning environment for a poly-cultural group of students is in a classroom where the teacher uses direct teaching methods, interacting with a class group that has been formed into a working group for purposes peculiar to the school.

Transition from the Child-Adult Relationship to the Peer Relationship. Here we find a great advantage in the direct teaching technique involving teacher-group interaction and teacher-individual interaction. It is not necessary to change the method of teaching as the interest of the child shifts from teacher to peers. Before the shift takes place the student seeks teacher approval which is displayed before the other students. After the shift takes place the students seek peer approval which is displayed before the teacher. So, we conclude, that direct instruction in the group setting is appropriate to both situations.

Chapter 4

Research Results and the New Theory

The Rand Report. "Research has not identified a variant of the existing system that is consistently related to student's educational outcomes." This is the principal finding of the "Rand Report" (1972). When Casper Weinberger was Secretary of HEW, the President's Commission on School Finance asked the Rand Corporation to make a study to determine what was then known regarding the determinants of educational effectiveness. The Rand Report was the result. The study was organized around five categories: (1) the input - output approach (19 major studies, including Coleman, 1966), (2) the process approach (effects of teachers and instruction, and student characteristics), (3) the organizational approach (study of eight major studies, which included size of system, rigidness of system, effect of the principal, use of lay input, influence of federal aid on organization, etc.), (4) the experimental approach (studies deal mostly with such subjects as student-teacher relations, parent-organization relations, student-society relations, etc.), and (5) evaluation of broad educational interventions (ESEA Title I, Head Start, Follow Through, Higher Horizons, and published evaluations of the intervention programs) (Averich, 1972).

The Response is Violent. At the time of the publication of the Rand report the education world was responding rather violently to the evaluation reports that were coming out. It became a national pastime to point to the inadequacies of the research, the flaws in design, the bias of the researcher, the wrong conclusions from the data presented, and the poor selection of statistical method. Writers and speakers seem to have concluded that the researchers were saying that "schools do not make a difference," an idea that could well lead the public to refuse to support public education. The trauma has subsided somewhat with leaders searching the reports to salvage what they can to insure the continued public support for educational research and public education.

A Shift to Qualitative Measures. The director of the National Institute of Education, Edward A. Curran, in a major paper presented to the annual meeting of the American Educational Research Association, March 1982, said: "The effective schools research has shown that properly run schools can improve the academic performance of any youngster. More specifically, it has shown that we can teach *any* child who comes through the door and that we know *how* to teach him. Still more specifically, a number of effective schools studies show that the *qualitative* differences in schools, based on tests of basic skills, can be accounted for by five factors:

1. strong leadership by the principal,
2. an orderly school climate conducive to learning
3. emphasis on basic skills
4. teacher expectations of high student achievement
5. a system of assessing student performance."

As Dr. Curran points out, these are *qualitative* differences. Qualitative differences are quite difficult to measure, or they are inferred from the results (Curran, 1982).

The Failure of Federal Efforts to Improve Education. It has not been easy for the Office of Education and/or the Department of Education to determine how it can influence or improve education in the United States. There is the basic assumption that the federal government can influence educational outcome by funding research. Over a twenty year period they have changed from emphasis on research and development centers in universities (the writer was director of one of these in the last two years of its existence 1968–70) to regional laboratories under private control, to centralized control by the National Institute of Education in Washington. There seems to be little evidence that the organization plan at the top makes much difference. The Rand Corporation is making a study of federal programs designed to introduce and spread innovative practices in public schools. Rand is attempting to identify what tends to promote various kinds of changes in schools and what doesn't. After completing the study of four programs (ESEA Title III, Innovative projects; ESEA Title VII, Bilingual Projects; Vocational Education Act, Exemplary Programs; and Right-to-Read Program) they concluded: "Neither the technology nor the project resources nor the different federal management strategies influenced outcomes in major ways," and that the main factors affecting innovations were in the institutional setting (Berman, April 1975).

If millions of dollars had been spent on many studies in the physical sciences over a period of twenty-five years and the results were largely neutral, the scientists would conclude that they were operating from no theory, or that the theories were so inappropriate that it amounted to "no theory." No theory produces random studies or the units used in the studies are randomly selected. Therefore, we expect random results.

The Missing Factor is a Viable Theory. A few writers have been telling us that we have no theory. Jerome R. Bruner, in 1968, wrote in the Saturday Review: "Despite the books and articles that are beginning to appear on the subject, the process of education goes forward today without any clearly defined or widely accepted theory of instruction. We have had to make do on clever maxims and moralistic resolutions about what instruction is and should be (Bruner, 1968)." John Goodlad, writing about his extensive research "A Study of

Schooling in the United States" wrote that he was asked "What is your theory of schooling? I answered that we were not using one because no adequate or useful one exists. To the question, what hypotheses are you testing? I answered, we're hoping to come up with some good ones (Goodlad, 1977)." Donald P. Sanders, in the Educational Researcher, March 1981, wrote: "In the United States, we now have had more than two decades of experience in this enterprise. Billions of dollars have been spent by government and private agencies in deliberate efforts to improve educational practices and operations. The effort has endured long enough so that it is possible to discern some of its effects, and unfortunately they are more than disappointing. Two primary conclusions have been drawn from the American experience: (1) the *expected* educational improvements have not ensued: and (2) on the other hand *unexpected* consequences result in undesirable changes in the school system. The first of these conclusions is rather well established (Gross, 1977)." Dr. Sanders, quoting Gross writes:

> "When systematic evaluations (of deliberate efforts to change the schools) have been made, the findings reveal that the intended outcomes generally were not achieved . . . for those projects in which success was claimed, a careful examination of their outcomes generally showed their results to lack statistical significance. . . . Furthermore, nearly every systematic study of the fate of a specific educational innovation in public schools has concluded that it's anticipated outcomes were not achieved, that it's educational benefits were minimal, or that it was not fully implemented (Gross, 1979 p. 10)."

Dr. Sanders elaborating on the second point (that innovations resulted in undesirable changes) wrote:

> It seems that a science that is inadequate as a guide to educational practice is being used to control and manage schooling. . . . Why has educational science reached this state? . . . Furthermore, there has been a persistent tendency in educational research to pursue limited descriptive or experimental studies without a complementary effort to develop

what Suppes (1974) called "deep running theory." ... It seems to me that a fundamental void exists at the heart of our concerns in educational science: we lack a scientific paradigm adequate for understanding and systematically investigating the process of educating. Our research has been excessively atheoretical and has not produced an accumulating body of systematically observed empirical facts. We lack both adequately testable theories of educating and the facts necessary to test or falsify them. (Sanders, 1981).

The Preponderance of Hierarchical Schemes is Evidence of the Absence of Viable Theory. Prime evidence of the absence of theory is the ubiquitous use of hierarchical schemes in all areas and phases of education. The history of the search for scientific knowledge is replete with examples of the fact that social pressure for improvement produces excessive use of reductionism, all kinds of classification systems, and subdividing the little knowledge that exists to absurd limits. These schemes often take on a developmental structure, and are often called "theories."

Hierarchical Schemes in Ancient Medicine. The writer owns Volume XI of an ancient encyclopedia which contains an extensive section on medicine. Paraphrasing the introduction: "The latest theory of medicine is expressed in the book: *Conspectus Medicinae Theoreticae* - by Dr. James Gregory, a professor of medicine at the University of Edinburgh - first published in 1780 and revised in 1782. Dr. Gregory begins by stating that some functions of the human body relate to *itself only* and others to *external things*, the latter being called *animal functions* and the former are called *natural* functions. A disease takes place when the body has so far declined from a sound state, that its functions are either *impeded* or *performed with difficulty*. A disease therefore may happen to any part of the body either *solid* or *liquid*, or to any one of the functions, or those may occur either *single* or *several of them joined together*; whence the distinction of diseases into *simple* or *com-*

pound. Most simple diseases are either *productive of others* or *of symtoms*. The causes of disease are often obscure or totally unknown. There are *proximate causes* and *remote causes*. Remote causes may be *predispondent* or *exciting* causes. . ." This line of "reasoning" continues for some three hundred large pages with the only impression being extreme admiration for Dr. Gregory's ability to produce such an elaborate scheme from so little data. (Already cited in Chapter Two is Aristotle's extended discussion of the elements: earth, water, air, and fire by playing them against hot, cold, wet, and dry.)

Hierarchical Schemes of Development Are Not Substitutes for Viable Theory. Educational leaders and pedagogical experts who design systems of schooling should resolve for themselves the serious questions posed by Phillips and Kelly concerning hierarchical theories of development published in the Harvard Educational Review of August, 1975 (Phillips, 1975). They review the works of Piaget and Inhelder, Kohlberg, Jensen, Erikson, and Gagne, and maintain that it is unclear whether their theories are empirically or conceptually grounded. They suggest that "the relationship between the levels is an implicative one, that is, if by definition the higher levels presuppose the existance of the lower ones" they are consequently not subject to empirical examination. "The concluding statement is as follows: It may well be unfair to claim that development theories are part folklore and part science, but it is not unfair to point out that a good many of the assumptions that have crept into modern developmental psychology are dubious." And quoting Kessen (1966) the authors write:

> The danger that our conclusions about the development of human knowledge may derive in large measure from the preconceptions of the nature of man and the nature of reality that we stuffed—or worse, let slip—into our initial construction of the psychological task (a danger that I believe to be clear and present in all current attempts to understand cognitive development) requires that we take a long uncom-

fortable look at our governing presuppositions (Kessen, 1966).

The Test is Usefulness, Not Unity or Coherence. It would seem quite obvious that it is theory that gives unity and coherence to any endeavor. But unity and coherence is not the major requirement. Usefulness is the major requirement. An implicative hierarchy would have unity and coherence built in. The question is: Do school instructional programs built on these hierarchical theories cause children to learn more? There is practically no evidence that they do. The writer was director of the campus laboratory school at Florida State University for most of the decade of the 50's. We were steeped in developmental psychologies, but he could see little in the day to day operation that reflected those theories. He was director of the Research and Development Center on Educational Stimulation at the University of Georgia (1968–70) trying to write curricula based on early learning (3-year-olds). We were Piagetian and Gagneian. If these hierarchical theories were of practical help he could not discover it.

The Lack of Direction Among Education Experts Reflects the Absence of Viable Theory. If there were any recognized theory or theories in the field of education the writings of the accepted experts and authorities should reflect the fact. Congressman Roman C. Pucinski, Chairman of the General Subcommittee on Education of the Committee on Education and Labor (Ninety-first Congress) in 1970, carried out an extensive project designed to give direction to the U.S. government's efforts to improve the schools of America (Pucinski 1970). The report of this project is 135 papers (29 reports of witnesses questioned by the committee, and 106 papers sent to the committee) from leading educators, influential people interested in education, and university professors. The report is remarkable in that very few great or near great were left out. One would expect such a compendium to be a veritable storehouse of knowledge and wisdom concerning the improvement of education. The effect is the exact opposite. The publication reflects the confusion and lack of direction that would exist in an atheoretical enterprise. The writer was asked to contribute a paper to this publication. His paper, "We Need a Handbook," reflected his frustration at trying to direct a federally funded research and development center without sound theory. He called for the production of a handbook that would concentrate in one publication what is solidly known in education upon which sound program could be built. It was suggested that such a handbook would cost from five to seven million dollars (Boyce, 1970). In 1974 the Goodyear Publishing Company did a repeat on the Subcommittee on Education's effort, but using only ten of the great names (Three were the same people that contributed to Congressman Pucinski's report). This book reflects the same confusion. (Hipple, 1974).

We Are Trying to Operate Without Viable Theory. The neutral results of twenty-five years of research and major intervention projects, the preponderance of hierarchical "theories" as a basis for instruction and curriculum, and the lack of any common direction in the writing of education experts, almost forces the conclusion that we are trying to operate without viable theory.

The Strength of the New Theory. It is in this context that the new theory is at its maximum strength. New theory should give a logical explanation of the data that led to the confusion and frustration in that field of study. The data was not gathered within the context of the new theory, but this is normal in theory development. New theory by its very nature must make new interpretations of old data. The data frustrates the educator because attempts to improve students' measured achievement by the manipulation of organization, teaching method, and/or curriculum, proved disappointing. Further analyses led to the examination of student characteristics. This led to the conclusion that the factors related to achievement were largely outside the school, and to factors not under the control of school personnel.

The Production Model is Identified (the TYPE THREE SCHOOL). The new theory, being based on the assumption that motivation to learn is a social/societal/cultural phenomenon directs attention to the nature (social) of the factors that are highly correlated with student achievement, and away from the location (outside the school) of those factors. We then may generalize the idea and say, "Motivation to learn is a social phenomenon whether it is exercised in school or out." If we look at the two dimensional description of the school (see Chapter 3) which is the new basic theory of schooling, we see an explanation of the decline in student achievement.

If we had assumed that the students' motivation is related to the values of the culture of which the student is a part (TYPE ONE SCHOOL), and we know that our school is a part of a poly-cultural society, we realize that the theory precludes this motivational base. If we had assumed that we have TYPE TWO motivation, in which the student is presumed to desire something the school has to offer, and we have a significant number of students who do not fit this category, we are faced with the probability that the theory has denied us this type of motivation. Having been denied TYPE ONE and TYPE TWO, we are left with TYPE THREE which makes motivation a property of the school itself. It is presumed that this describes the present condition of education. If this analysis is justified, then it is this setting that has produced the non-results described at the beginning of the chapter. This is also the production/factory model identified by John I. Goodlad in his first report on "A Study of Schooling (Goodlad, 1979)." He writes, "The prevailing production model of schooling is powerful and seductive; it will be around for a long time to come . . . it is a weak predictor of what is likely to happen when interventions designed to increase productivity are injected into the system. We endeavored, therefore, to eschew as much as possible the production model and the assumptions accompanying it . . . In rejecting the theoretical perspective from which this model stems, we substitute no clearly delineated alternative theory (Goodlad, 1979)." It is interesting to note that Dr. Goodlad concluded from his extensive research in schools that efforts are being made to force the production/factory model onto the school setting, and that he has come to reject this model as inappropriate. The writer, in the original theory paper, projected the production/factory model as a logical consequence of the theory (Boyce 1976).

Can Strong Group Motivation be Generated Inside the School? If the new theory is now seen as providing a logical "explanation" of the present state of education, and accounts for the neutral results from research on projects designed to improve student achievement; we now must face the critical question of whether the factors correlated with student achievement are *necessarily* outside the school, or if social factors can be generated *within* the school with enough strength to significantly affect student achievement in a genuinely polycultural society, a society in which all people of school age are presumed to be in school.

This question will have to be answered by the reader based on the perceived logic and internal consistency of the plan for schooling presented here. This plan is designed to move the strong motivational forces inherent in social groups from *outside the school* to *inside the school*. An overview of the plan follows in Chapter 5.

Chapter 5

An Overview of the New School

The Short-Term and Long-Term Goals of the New School. As stated in Chapter Two, the new school will have a single short-term goal: to provide, in a society in which all adults are expected to work, a wholesome, healthy, disciplined place for children and youth. The new school will have a single long-term goal which is to produce maximum literacy in the pre-adult population. Maximum literacy means the extension of literacy both vertically and horizontally. Vertically means the extension of literacy to as high a level as possible. Horizontally means literacy in as many areas as possible. This chapter presents an overview of a school that could achieve, to a reasonable degree, these short and long-term goals while assuming that motivation to learn is a social phenomenon. We do not claim that the proposed plan is the only plan that could meet these requirements nor that it is the best that could be conceived. Nor do we claim that all parts of the plan are absolutely necessary. The purpose of this discussion is to show that all parts of the school must contribute to the central purposes of the school. It is unfortunate that many school practices that are now deemed highly desirable by a large number of educators are not possible if we are to be true to the new theoretical approach. The overview of the school naturally involves the school organization which should normally be derived from the curriculum and method of instruction. It seems appropriate at this point to give a general organizational plan, since the organizational structure is necessarily quite different from the familiar present-day school.

The Four Levels of the New School. Membership in each of the four levels of schooling is determined strictly by chronological age. It is assumed that the public school system is established for all pre-adults (until 18 years of age) beginning at age two. The four levels are also determined by chronological age: *Early School* for 2, 3, 4, and 5 year-olds; *Primary School* for 6, 7, 8, and 9 year-olds; *Middle School* for 10, 11, 12, and 13 year-olds; and *Secondary School* for 14, 15, 16, and 17 year-olds (until age 18).

The Four Units of the New School. Each level of the school system will consist of four units. Of course, there will be adjustments appropriate to the age of the children or youth of each level. No one of the four units is to be "adjusted out" as not being appropriate to that level. Each unit is essential at all levels. The following description of the four units assumes a 10 year-old student. The four units are: (1) *The Medical Center*, (2) *The School Base*, (3) *The Dramatic Arts Center*, and (4) *The Basic Literacy Center.*

The Medical Center: a Description. This center is basically a hospital and clinic for children and youth. The personnel consists of: pediatricians, nurses, and special service personnel. It is presumed that the next major development in the area of federally sponsored medical service will be a complete program for children and youth. The physical location for such a program will be in the public school if the school is structured to make such a move possible and reasonable. The medical center is a hospital for children or youth that is run by a husband and wife team of pediatricians. It is also the base of the special service personnel who function as did special education teachers, but without teaching responsibility. This center is maintained 24 hours a day every day of the year.

The Medical Center and the Short-Term Goal of the School. If it is presumed that all parents work (hold paying jobs) there must be a place for children and youth while they work. This is well understood for the very young children. It is not so clearly recognized for the youth. But the whole society cries out for a wholesome place for older youth. For this kind of service to children and youth, the tie-in with a federal health program is essential.

The Medical Center and the Long-Term Goal of the School. The connection between physical well-being and school achievement is no longer debatable. In any system of schooling that claims equal opportunity, the health service is essential. Basic to learning is the attitude toward life in general. A critical factor in learning for the disadvantaged is the syndrome of uncertainty about continued life and health, and attitude toward the probability of death or disease.

The School Base: a Description. The school base, like the medical center, is a 24 hour-a-day operation. It is under the supervision of a husband and wife team of retirement age. The two are called "pedagogues." They are chosen for wisdom and stability and not for some professional competence. They serve as mediators between the various school personnel and the students and between the school and the home. The school base consists of an apartment for the pedagogues, limited overnight facilities for students, space for students with tables for a class group, individual toilets and washrooms, showers, work space, and lockers.

The School Base and the Short-Term Goal of the School. The school base is not a home base. The pedagogue is not a quasi-parent nor a parent substitute. Parents and home assume that the services of the mediator are always in operation at the school setting. The school base is the location from which the student operates, as an individual and as a part of a class group (probably 30 students). This school base makes the elongated day possible, providing both privacy and group relationships. With the medical service, the school base provides a wholesome place for children or youth while parents work.

The School Base and the Long-Term Goal of the School. The school base makes it possible for the teacher to give full attention to the teaching function. The existence of this base, with the pedagogue-mediator, permits the basic literacy component to be quite formal. With the services of the dramatic arts center, the school base permits intensive work by the teacher for the full class period of basic literacy development.

The Dramatic Arts Center: a Description. The personnel of this center consist of a director of dramatic arts who is in charge of the whole program of the center. Other personnel are: (1) directors of musical arts, (2) directors of fine arts, and (3) directors of physical arts. The center is to produce a performance involving all students, for parents and public, every six weeks. The work of the center is to build each class unit into a working group involving the whole school for support.

The Dramatic Arts Center and the Short-Term Goal of the School. This unit of the school provides for primary and basic needs of children or youth necessary for a full and satisfying life, including the need to be part of a group, as well as the need for an outlet of energy through vigorous physical activity. Needs are met for self-expression through art, music, physical activity, and drama. The existence of this center relieves the teacher of basic literacy of serving this same basic need, and permits more intense concentrated effort in the literacy classes.

The Dramatic Arts Center and the Long-Term Goal of the School. This unit, with the medical service, furnishes the key element in the new school. The primary purpose of the dramatic arts center is to build the class groups and the whole school into a primary social unit. The class group (approximately 30 students) is built by the application of visceral forces that have always built and maintained primary social units: concerted body movement, group music, and art. School unity is built in the periodic presentations by all students. The basic literacy unit depends upon the dramatic arts center to build the class unit into a group, approximating a primary social group as nearly as possible with the means at its disposal. It is assumed that the class unit arrives at the basic literacy center as a group, feeling that they are a group, and that the teacher can maintain the group through group instruction. It is also assumed that the basic literacy teacher cannot build a poly-cultural group into a school group without the work of dramatic arts and the medical center.

The Basic Literacy Center: a Description. The personnel of this center are teachers (the term "teacher" is used only in this center). This is a formal place where there is only one type of activity. These activities are *directly* related to the teaching and the learning of the basic languages of English, history, geography, mathematics, biology and physical science. The other units of the school are valuable in their own right, and make primary contributions to life and society. But, the primary purpose of these other units is to give support to the long-term goal of the school. The focus of this purpose is in the basic literacy center. In this center are teachers who have a private classroom, a teacher's office and a private washroom. In the classroom are the tools of the teacher's trade. The primary tools are books, primary references, dictionaries, atlases, maps, globes, etc. A notable absence of machines for teaching such as T.V., movie projectors, overhead projectors, and an absence of books written for students and teachers. There *are* machines for the first steps in book production. Essential to the operation is a modern, fast, copying machine.

The Basic Literacy Center and the Short-Term Purpose of the School. If parents are to work and feel free to give their full attention to their work during the working day, they need to feel that their children are learning, and that what the children are learning is understandable to parents. They need assurance that what they are learning is as basic as reading, writing, and arithmetic. The existence of this formal place, in itself, gives such assurance. What is taking place can be *seen*. Teachers are seen actively teaching. There is a daily product that can be examined by parents. This kind of assurance is as important as the medical center in establishing the school as a "safe, wholesome place for children or youth."

The Basic Literacy Center and the Long-Term Goal of the School. This center is, of course, the focus of the long-term goal of the school.

Chapter 6

School Practice that Inhibits the Effectiveness of the New Theory

The Problem of Poly-Cultural Education Defined. It is a central thesis of this book that students resist learning what the school teaches when the student does not perceive that he/she is a full member of a group that holds as a primary value what is to be learned. Those educators who hold that education should work from the interests or felt needs of the student would be hard pressed to justify teaching a non-reading culture to read. Yet in the cross-cultural or the poly-cultural school we have chosen to make all non-adults literate in several areas of knowledge. The new theory helps us to understand that this is a very difficult undertaking, and shows the necessity for structuring a group-building curriculum (the dramatic arts unit) and a group-sustaining method (group instruction in the basic literacy unit) in order to achieve this end. This school based group or school culture cannot be strong enough to replace the cultural forces outside the school. It is believed, however, that the school can concentrate on one cultural attribute (literacy) and produce results if the school avoids suggesting that total cultural restructing is necessary. So, it should be clear that the theory defines the problem, and shows why the complex social approach is necessary. Since the long-term goal of the school puts major strain on the group-developing capacity of the school, it is necessary to reduce to a minimum all other school activities that tend selectively to attract identifiable groups that have their base outside the school, or that in themselves produce groupings that have a contrary influence. Such activities would (according to the new theory) destroy the environment that permits and encourages the achievement of the long-term goal of the school.

The Elective System. Choice of courses always produces a cultural/social polarization of the student body. This is often considered a desirable end in the present-day schools in that the "desirable" subjects tend to not attract "undesirable" students. The new school proposes to *deal with* the basic social problems of the poly-cultural school, rather than *hide* the problems under an elective system.

Vocational Education. Vocational subjects, as electives, share the problems described in the paragraph above. The effect is greater, however, than that produced by the choice between academic subjects. However, the state should provide vocational training for the non-adult, but vocational training should be reserved for the highly motivated student. In vocational training the students should be treated as adults and trained "on-the-job" or in highly specialized schools. School officials should not expect that vocational training can be effectively used to motivate students to achievement in basic skills such as reading and writing.

Grouping Students by Ability or Achievement. It seems quite obvious that grouping socially polarizes students. The educator will ask whether the trade-off is worth it. The assumption in the new school is that maintaining the group is paramount.

Interscholastic Athletics. Twenty-five years ago the writer would have attempted to use the spirit generated in an athletic program to promote the goals of the school. At that time he was director of a campus laboratory school that had a well-coordinated physical education and athletic program. But under the light of the new theory he realizes that the laboratory school was a TYPE TWO SCHOOL in that the students chose (or their parents chose for them) to attend. The school was poly-cultural in only a most superficial respect. In today's school, the athletic program seems to be the ultimate as a divider of students into groups and cultures.

Male and Female Groups. This has been the hardest point for the writer to deal with. It forced itself to the scene as a direct result of consistent pursuit of the theory. The extensive study of the sociology of groups and cultures has made it clear that the male-female role characteristic may be the strongest cultural identification there is. The school could easily and unconsciously give support to a dominant group in spite of its efforts to build a culturally neutral school environment. Data relevant to this important problem seems to be non-existent. The new school should avoid this cultural trap and refuse to establish activities that divide male and female students. The single literacy curriculum does not polarize sexually. There would be no problem in music and art. The physical art directors would have to depart markedly from tradition. The physical activities envisioned by the writer are not sexually oriented. Many of the activities should be quite vigorous and directed toward the development of strong bodies. The female should not be exempt from this. Concerns that are necessarily sexual (involving sexual organs) are dealt with in private by the medical personnel.

The Gang Toilet. The gang school toilet has long been the meeting place of gangs of all kinds, usually to the detriment of the school. In the new school, toilet facilities, as well as dressing facilities, are private and located in the school base. In an emergency the student could use the private toilet of the teacher or director.

The School Lunchroom. If the central lunchroom could be avoided it would be a great advantage. It is hoped that a system can be devised for serving a snack at the school base two or three times a day and permitting students to bring their snacks from home. The medical unit will need to keep a record of the food consumption of each student, but it should be recognized that the student's primary food intake is outside the school. It seems that a serious program designed to record the total food intake would be more effective than a school effort to supplement or compensate for an inadequate diet. The nature and character of the method of food consumption is so clearly culturally based that the school should generate its own pattern of food consumption. To avoid social polarization, this method should be purely utilitarian, consistent with the "busy" environment generated at school.

Chapter 7

The New Theory and the New Curriculum

Curriculum for Basic Literacy. The new school will have a single long-term purpose which is to produce maximum literacy in the pre-adult population. Maximum literacy means the extension of literacy both vertically and horizontally. Vertically means the extension of literacy to as high a level as possible. Horizontally means literacy in as many areas as possible. A literacy area is defined as a dimension of knowledge that has its own basic language. We can no longer afford to identify basic literacy in restricted terms as if an ability to read can be generalized into all fields. "Ability to read," in the current usage of the term, does not mean that the person can read chemistry, or algebra, or geography any more than "ability to count" means that the person can determine the monthly payments on a $14\frac{1}{2}$% loan over a 12 month period.

Dr. Kenneth Levine, the noted British sociologist, writing on functional literacy in a recent issue of the *Harvard Educational Review* says:

> To put it quite simply, if we are interested in the broader national and international ramifications of literacy, we must consider the application and exercise of reading and writing skills to specific bodies and types of information. Literacy cannot be reduced to the question of the fluency with which an individual is capable of reading a newspaper. . . . We cannot afford to ignore the content and functions of written

47

materials; the information they contain is a strategic social resource. The possession or lack of particular kinds of information constitutes a crucial component in the opportunities—or "life chances"—open to social classes; a channel of information is part of each apparatus of social domination (Levine, 1982).

In attempting to expand the idea of what is basic to being functionally literate in the modern age, we have selected six areas that supply the basic languages to most fields of study. A list of six areas is not difficult to identify: (1) English, (2) history, (3) geography, (4) mathematics, (5) physical science, and (6) biology. Many arguments can no doubt be made for extending the list; however, the necessity of keeping the number small and simply stated without elaborate titles will become clear as the complete plan unfolds. Defining these areas in terms of language directs attention to the continuing developmental nature of the "subject" and to the necessity of continuing instruction in each area for the full span of the early, primary, middle, and secondary school experience. A notable omission is the foreign language. This is left out, because it is doubtful that a single foreign language could be agreed upon. A single basic curriculum for all students is essential to the new theory. An elective language program would weaken the system. In the literacy section of the curriculum the emphasis is on "the languages of English, the languages of mathematics," etc. The single long-term purpose of the school is "student literacy" which is directly taught in six literacy building areas.

Curriculum for Group-Building. A second section of the curriculum has as its purpose the building of the students into strong groups. The curriculum for group-building is: (1) physical arts (2) fine arts, and (3) musical arts. These three are brought together in a dramatic arts center. If the place of the three group-building areas in the curriculum is understood, the reader has come a long distance toward the understanding of the proposed theory.

The Medical Service as Curriculum. The neat classification of areas into literacy-building and group-building breaks down at a most critical point: where to place the medical service in the logical scheme. In order to appreciate the theory, it is important to remember that this proposal is for a school in poly-cultural society where every school-aged person is in school, and in a society where it is assumed that all adults work. This means that we strive for a single common school in which there is no preferred social group. The new theory calls attention to a set of facts that are known correlates with school achievement but have been largely ignored because of the difficulty of fitting the implied solutions into the present school structures. This set of facts is associated with and are factors in the loosely structured term: "socio-economic-status" (SES). This is a part of the basis for the tenet, inherent in the theory, "that motivation to learn is a social phenomenon."

The most universally ignored implication has to do with the basic health and nutrition of the learner, and the attitude toward learning in children that is the result of uncertainty about disease, life, and death. Any public plan for schooling in the United States that claims to deal with the conditions that gave rise to the new theory, which does not have as a major concern the general health of the child, would have to be branded as totally political, insincere, or based on ignorance. It is the proposed theory that directs attention to the general health of the child because of its relation to the identity problem of depressed children and their self-image. This is so important to the child's willingness to invest in formal education over a long period of time. It is presumed that this ingredient is automatically supplied to the children in upper and middle class groups. This may be why its importance is not generally recognized by those responsible for setting educational policy.

As has been previously pointed out, the medical service is also essential in achieving the short-term purpose of the school, that of providing in a society in which all adults are expected to work, a wholesome, healthy, disciplined place for children and youth. To provide such a service, it is obvious that school must admit two-year-olds, and that a medical service must be provided. A reason for including the medical service in the curriculum chapter is the general belief by the public that the school should "teach" subjects that combat the major social problems of children and youth. It is the assumption here that such teaching programs are largely ineffective, and that they cannot be effectively taught in the usual sense of the word. Such programs properly fit into a general health and medical program such as would be supplied in a complete medical service. The physical education program would be closely allied with the medical service, as would the nutrition program.

Basic Literacy, or Language and the Lingua Franca. It seems necessary at this point to offer an apology for the failure of the theory to support the comprehensive school which has come to be the ideal in American public education. It was decided early in the development of the new theory that there was no way to relate the new theory to the comprehensive school with its many ability and achievement streams and its wide offering of subjects, many of which are perceived as career and vocational, as well as terminal in nature. It may have been the writer's experience in Africa that produced the first glimmer of the new theory of schooling. The state school systems of developing countries had grown from either a missionary school system or a colonial school system. Whatever the expressed purpose of the school, whether vocational, professional or academic, the writer became convinced that the students came to school to learn to read and write, at a high level, the language of commerce (*the lingua franca*). This is also probably the source of the idea to place basic education in the language mode.

The Whole Curriculum is Continuous. Each area of curriculum is maintained continuously from the time the child enters school until the youth becomes an adult at eighteen, ready for a job, or ready for post-secondary education. One reason for putting the basic literacy part of the curriculum in the "language mode" is to stress the importance of the continuous nature of the program. The most widely read and probably the most influential education book of modern times is Jerome Bruner's *The Process of Education*. The book is a short report on a conference of leading educators and scholars who were discussing new educational methods that were being evolved largely under the auspices of the National Academy of Sciences in the new curriculum movement. Dr. Bruner's opening statement of the "Readiness for Learning" chapter is as follows:

> We begin with the hypothesis that any subject can be taught effectively in some intellectually honest form to any child at any stage of development. It is a bold hypothesis and an essential one in thinking about the nature of a curriculum. No evidence exists to contradict it; considerable evidence is being amassed that supports it. (Bruner, 1960 p. 33)

Operating under the old theory (Bruner later contended that there was no theory), the statement supported strictly sequenced curriculum written by subject field experts, which led eventually to the individualized program for each child. Under the new theory the Bruner statement supports the continuous curriculum concept.

The Curricuum Summarized. The curriculum of the new school is conceived as existing in two parts: (1) a literacy-building part in which the languages of English, history, geography, mathematics, physical science, and biology are taught; and (2) a group-building part utilizing physical arts, fine arts, and musical arts, separately, and regularly combining the three for special programs. Both parts are supported by a complete medical program for children and youth, the purpose being the maintenance of a high level of health, the treatment of disease, and building medically centered programs that deal with those social problems of children and youth that are, under the present system of education, considered proper parts of the school's curriculum. All parts of the curriculum are maintained continuously throughout the period of pre-adult schooling.

Chapter 8

The New Theory Calls for New Teaching Methods

Failure to Learn and Group Identity. When we state that motivation to learn is a social phenomenon we are suggesting that learning is, in some way, related to some group structure. If the school, or what is taught at school, is consistent with the values, ideals, and hopes of the group of which the student is a part, under the new theory, no major problems of learning are anticipated. It is also assumed that if what is taught is not endemic in the student's primary group, we may expect all kinds of learning problems to arise. There is always, however, a small group who will use school learning to break out of the primary group and become socially mobile. Under normal social conditions this group is very small because of the perceived permanent loss of the security that is basic to the person's existence and survival. In this social model, failure to learn means that the material to be learned has been identified by the student as belonging to a group that is foreign, strange, or even hostile to that student, and that cooperating with the school in learning that material may be interpreted as a rejection of the student by his/her primary group.

Two Ways to Combat Resistance to Learning. There are two ways, suggested by the logic of the social description of the student's motivation, to reduce the trauma produced by the student's feeling that any identification with competing

53

groups will produce rejection by the primary group or a lowered social status within the group: (1) produce a competing group that supplies the necessary security and provides the means of transition to that new group; (2) provide in a school setting, a new group which will furnish the needed group security while the student is in the school but does not suggest that the new group relationship be transported outside to the territory of the old group. The new school operates in the second category (setting up a school-centered group) with the expectation that the school group will eventually supply the basic security needs of the student, making the outside group unnecessary. For those who enter the school setting at age two, it is anticipated that the groups that could compete with the school values (what is taught at school) would not develop in the first place.

Not a Single American Culture. It is not in the interest of the school to produce a single American culture. Such an idea would not be acceptable in our nation. It is a purpose of the school to prevent the formation of values within cultures that are inimical to learning the languages essential to living a full life in a technical and scientific society. Major questions posed by the new theory are: can a central purpose for schooling be identified that is appropriate to a society that places great value on its diversity, and can a school be so structured that it maintains a sharp focus on that purpose without continuously producing cultural or group conflict? An industrial world problem of a similar nature was effectively addressed in a massive study by Geert Hofstede (Hofstede, 1980). Hofstede's study was concerned with finding the most effective organization for a large multi-national or international industry operating in 40 different modern nations. In each nation there were at least two cultures which made up the administration and management. At least one of these cultures was considered to be foreign. When top management is foreign (we will call it American to facilitate discussion), is it wise to try to educate the local management to American ways, or do the Americans try to adjust the management model to the local situation? A major finding was that neither produces the most efficient organization; and that two or more cultures can and do rally around the central purpose of the organization if it is made a major concern of management; if it is specifically planned for, and if the people are not expected to carry the inter-cultural relationship into other aspects of their lives. Dr. Hofstede states it as follows:

> Creating the organization's own subculture is a vitally important task of the management of any organization, but even more in those organizations dealing with cultural diversity among their own members. . . . Organizational subcultures arise around task-relevant issues. A shared company subculture between people of otherwise different national cultures considerably facilitates communication and motivation. In general, we find that outstandingly successful organizations usually have strong and unique subcultures; the successes themselves contribute to the company mythology which reinforces the subculture. (Hofstede, 1980, pp. 393–394).

A Solution in a Multi-National Corporation. The best solution to the problem of maximum production in the international or multi-national corporation is to consecrate the multi-cultured company personnel to the purposes of the corporation (the production of the company product) without reference to the cultural diversity that exists outside. The purpose of the corporation is not "to solve the cultural differences" that exist within the company personnel, but to assure the maximum production of a known product. This is another way of saying that the motivation to produce the company product in a multi-cultural corporation is a social phenomenon.

A School Can Rally Around a Single School Purpose. If a school can abandon the idea that its purpose is to reshape the society by direct intervention through the students, we may be able to build a viable school. School people have held so long, and so intently, that if there are social problems to be solved, the student must practice solving these problems at school. If social decisions are to be made in the society, children at school must practice making these decisions at school. To attack or even question the validity of this sacred and clever "maxim" is considered treason (this clever maxim is, of course: "learn by doing"). But the major problem of solving such problems at school stems from the fact that it is impossible to introduce at school level the most important ingredient of the problem solving or decision making process; that of bearing the consequences of a poor decision. This approach to learning, if successful, tends to produce people who believe planning in a protected environment can produce solutions to major social problems. If the plan fails, it follows that the failure is due to "politics or to corrupt people."

What then must be the nature of the long-term purpose of the school? *It must be some essential ingredient of the social structure that can be contained within the bounds (territory) of the school, which can be intensively participated in by all students and does not force the individuals of the multi-cultural group to defend themselves in terms of their own identity based on the outside-the-school groups.* There is no way to avoid the fact that the cultural value of reading and writing as a basis for participation in the "good life" in America, has at present, a definite cultural identity. This does not relieve the school of the responsibility to find ways to "get around" the cultural resistance to a central literacy program in the schools. Neither does it mean that the schools must take on the reforming of the total social and economic structure as a prerequisite to acceptable student achievement in the many "languages" of the school program. The idea of basic literacy is expanded to areas of knowledge that have their own basic language. The single rallying point for the total school is the expressed long-term goal: to produce maximum literacy in the pre-adult population.

We Do Not Need to Wait for a Major Cultural Transformation. If we adopt the new theory of schooling and follow a logic based on that theory, it is no longer necessary to accept the Jerome Bruner conclusion ". . . for if the past decade has taught us anything, it is that educational reform confined only to the schools and not to the society at large is doomed to eventual triviality" (Bruner, 1968 p. 69). Dr. Bruner's conclusion is the logical one based on current theory. It is the new theory that gives new direction to schools which does not require that the school wait until the society-at-large undergoes some major transformation. Dr. Bruner's conclusion draws attention to the enormity of the problem and serves to remind us that the changes required must be of the same magnitude.

We have seen (in the curriculum chapter) that we need to give up the elective curriculum in order to sustain group identity over a long period of time. The need for group instruction in the physical arts, musical arts, and fine arts is made clear. These groups are doing things together in order to produce a unity in the group. These areas have been used for that purpose since the beginning of social activity in humans. This makes use of the most primary needs of people.

Maintaining the Group is a Limiting Factor in Teaching Method. The maintaining of the group in the school classes to promote literacy development would lose most of its effectiveness if the group interaction were not maintained in those areas. This requires that a major part of the instruction in these literacy areas be interaction between the teacher and the class and between the teacher and individuals in the class.

The Teacher, Not the Book, is the Authority Source. The teacher behaves as if he/she is author of the materials being learned (remember we are dealing with what is considered as basic in the several literacy areas). This means that the teacher must know what is being taught without constant reference to printed material on the subject. An ideal way to achieve this would be to perceive of the student as the *writer* of the book ("End with the book" instead of "Begin with the book"). A time at the end of each class period would be reserved for the student to write a summary page of what had been learned for the day. The page is identified in a routine way as to student, teacher, subject, date, etc. A copy would be made on a copying machine with the teacher filing the copy under the student's name. The original becomes a page of the book being developed by the student.

Individual Differences in Students. Since we are keeping a group of students together as long as possible, provision must be made for rather large differences in student achievement. Of importance in achieving this goal is the organization, or lack of organization, of the basic material in each literacy area (English, mathematics, history, geography, biology, and physical science). We assume that there is no beginning place for cognitive development (This may be part of the reason that great emphasis on mini-sequence has failed to produce the expected results). We then think in terms of islands of knowledge, or concentrations of knowledge, built around the people who made key contribution to that stream of knowledge through the ages. There would be a strong temptation to begin with pre-historic times and work forward in time—or begin with the present and work back to beginnings. This is to be avoided with a passion, or we will be back into sequential curriculum, and back to an organization plan that would force the dismemberment of the groups. The group must be maintained at all costs.

The group is maintained in physical arts, fine arts, and musical arts in which the purpose is to build the group. In the areas of instruction that promote basic literacy, the group must continue to be maintained. So, in describing the teaching method, we conclude that the first principle is the importance of the group. If the purpose in maintaining the group is understood, it follows that the class is constantly under the direction of the teacher. The teacher maintains a situation of interaction with the class as a whole, interspersed with interaction with the individual students. The difference in student ability and achievement is recognized by encouraging individual students to expand horizontally what is being learned, and adding to the individual's book the record and results of this learning. If the material learned in the class group is basic, one of its major characteristics is its expandability horizontally.

The Island of Knowledge. In the typical teaching session the teacher will introduce an island of knowledge which consists of a name and a related idea. The idea should be such that it can be reduced to a statement that can be learned (memorized, if you please) by the class as a group. This should be quite basic and a key to knowledge in the "language" being learned. This is then tied to the name of the person who conceived the idea or who developed it. This constitutes a unit that everyone in the class holds in common. It is reviewed in future sessions as if it were one of the ten commandments or a part of the multiplication table. The unit should be such that it is expandable both vertically and horizontally. Vertically to lead to other units for the whole group, and horizontally to form the basis for individual work. This island of knowledge, or unit, becomes a part of the written record that each student keeps, making a formal record at the end of each teaching session.

Units are Tagged in Time and Space. The brain is an instrument that seeks and relates knowledge. The brain will relate its new knowledge to previously learned knowledge if it can find a clue that permits it. A creative thinker is one whose brain does better than average in recognizing these clues. Instead of the teacher "explaining" the relationship to the student, the teacher provides the basic material learned with "tags" that make the process of relating possible. The system that seems to suit the brain best is the place of the idea in time and space. Each idea and person should be "located" in this manner. The student should build charts of time and space for pegging each idea and person. These charts should be constructed by the student as his/her knowledge grows. Commercially prepared schemes should not be used.

Explaining the Need, as Method, is Not Appropriate. When the assumption is made that the individuals in the class are part of a monolithic culture, and the teacher is part of that culture, it is appropriate to explain to the students why they should learn what is being taught (as in career education where the student is encouraged to select a profession or an area for his/her life's work). Then this choice by the student is used as a basis for "explaining" why the student needs to succeed in mastering the subject matter presented by the school. This system of motivation can be expected to work where the student shares the basic cultural values upon which the scheme is based. No such assumptions can be made in cross-cultural education. A major distinction between cultures is in the area of the culture's conception of what constitutes success, or the acceptable process through which success is achieved. Or, it may be that success in one culture may separate the individual from the group in another culture. Thus, we abandon the usual verbal arguments (apologies) for learning the material and turn to the major thesis of this book, that motivation to learn is a social phenomenon.

We Turn To Group (Social) Pressure. Since, under the new theory, we do not expect the normal pressures applied to the student (such as explaining the need for) to influence learning to work across cultures, we are left with direct group pressure as the instrument to induce learning. In military training this pressure is the norm. A group is trained together to risk their lives on command. They respond to the command "charge" (in the face of gunfire), not for love of country, or freedom, or family, but because of the group, and their unwillingness to expose their fear to the group. The writer has seen this group pressure in classes learning to speak English all over the world (many countries in Africa and in the USSR and China). A group is being instructed by a method in which the teacher repeats an English sentence; the class repeats it several times. Then the teacher asks individual students to repeat the sentence, which the student does. The teacher moves about the room and listens to the individuals in the group response. It seems that the teacher asks for the individual response only when the teacher is sure the student can do it. The writer saw one student hesitate when called on, and the whole class felt embarassed. The writer has heard American teachers identify this method of teaching as "rote memory" adding a disdainful smile. The writer calls it, in the light of the new theory, "social learning." There is wholesale agreement that language learning is a social process. It is the recent rise of cognitive psychology that has shown that the acquisition of knowledge is irrevocably tied to language development.*

Support from Cognitive Psychology. The teaching method described above might seem crude or undignified to American teachers except for the probability that when the basic import of the shift in psychology from the long domination of behaviorism, to giving major attention to cognitive processes is more fully understood, recognition of the importance of the social setting in initial learning experiences will be routine. The periodical *Psychology Today* produced its fifteenth anniversary issue in May 1982. The issue featured "State-of-the-Science" reports by eleven noted psychologists. These psychologists were to answer the question: "What have we started to learn about human psychology—the processes behind our behavior, perceptions, and beliefs—that we didn't know 15 years ago (Psychology Today, May 1982)." Jerome Bruner wrote:

> *The discussion from here to the end of the chapter is rather long. If the reader is willing to wade through it, it will be worth it, for it firmly establishes from research the legitimacy of the language mode as a basic learning structure, strongly supports direct instruction as a superior method of instruction, and generates a new theory of learning that supports the new theory and the new school.

I . . . see two related signs of growth. The first is the continued movement of psychology away from the restrictive
shackles of behaviorism toward a more flexible emphasis on
cognitive processes. The second is the increase in intellectual commerce between psychology and neighboring fields
that also study man. . . . Before (the 1950's) studies of men-
tal processes were considered eccentric, if interesting, defi-
nitely not in the mainstream of psychology. Afterward, the
"metaphor" of human thought became crucial. . . .

The change was not limited to American psychology. It
ranged from Russia (first inspired by Vygotsky and Luria),
through Switzerland (with the impetus of Piaget), through
Britain . . . to America (Bruner 1982).

Ulric Neisser was another contributor to the *Psychology Today* symposium. He is credited with being the first to make
the title of a book "Cognitive Psychology" 15 years ago (1967).
He writes:

It (cognitive psychology) has become a rival to psychoan-
alytically based psychology and to behaviorism. . . . Cognitive psychology, in contrast (to the above) conceives of men
and women as seekers after information, who can discover
truth, though they are not immune to error. It tries to understand how knowledge is possible; how we obtain information, order it, and use it; what we perceive and how we
conceive of it . . . moreover, all versions of cognitive psychology agree, at least implicitely, that people *choose* much
of what they know. The choices are made in many ways:
through selective attention, the application of cognitive
strategies, the acquisition of cognitive skills. But human
beings are not just the playthings of blind instict or the slaves
of repeated reinforcement. They can see, learn and understand. We have always known this about ourselves, but no
other approach to psychology has legitimized that knowledge and tried to deepen it (Neisser, 1982).

After discussing perceiving and imagining, in relation to the
individual's *choice*, Dr. Neisser continues:

Perceiving and imagining are not the only cognitive skills,
language is especially important for our conception of hu-

man nature because language is uniquely our own. . . . Failure of these intensive efforts (a reference to efforts to bestow sign language on apes) is even more impressive when it is contrasted with the naturalness and spontaneity of human language. Children all over the world learn an amazing variety of languages, all at about the same age and all without formal instruction . . . we tell each other the truth, or lies, or nothing; there is as much choice in speaking as perceiving. We cannot avoid these choices any more than we can avoid language itself—because we are human (Neisser, 1982).

Leslie A. Hart, author of the Proster Theory which was expounded in his book *How the Brain Works* (Basic Books, 1975), writing in the Phil Delta Kappan of February 1978, says:

The human brain is intensely aggressive. Each brain is highly individual, unique; it seeks out, demands, and will accept only what it needs next to "make sense" of surrounding reality, as it perceives that reality. . . . The brain is now seen to be by no means the stimulus-response device presented in various behaviorist theories. We now know beyond question that it is elaborately "gated." That is, it will admit only those inputs it decides to admit, and each brain processes what it does admit in its own individual way. As teachers soon discover, what is admitted may be sharply different from what the teacher intended. The processing depends little on what or how the teacher has presented, and greatly on the total, previous, stored experience in that particular brain. . . . Young students in particular must talk to learn well and rapidly, for a great portion of the human brain (unlike those of laboratory animals) is devoted to language. . . . We are obsessed by "logic," usually meaning by that term tight, step-by-step, ordered, sequential (linear) effort in verbal or symbolic form. Educators try to make the curriculum, the schedule, and teaching "logical." But the human brain has little use for logic of this kind (Hart 1978).

Earlier in this chapter Dr. Jerome Bruner was quoted as writing that the emphasis on cognitive process was first inspired by Vygotsky and Luria (Bruner, 1982). The recognition of the work of L. S. Vygotsky (1896–1934) and his student and successor Alexander R. Luria has come late in the English speaking world—probably due to our preoccupation with behaviorism and the tendency to downgrade psychological work done in the USSR by labeling it as Marxist. Both men did, as is expected in the USSR, seek support of their ideas in the writings of Marx and Lenin.

The problem of the voluntary act on the part of the child has been a major block in the history of psychology, because the voluntary act on the part of the child was considered outside the scientific paradigm. Therefore, if a child seemed to commit an act of the will, it was necessary to explain it *out* of the study process. Vygotsky freed himself to objectively study this seeming phenomenon by applying to this area the same system of thought that enabled Galileo and Newton to objectively study and analyze the free-falling body. Whether there could be a voluntary act was considered a philosophical question, outside the realm of objective science (and psychology has tried hard to be scientific). Vygotsky decided to study this seeming phenomenon, concentrating on the "how," leaving the idealistic question of "why" to the philosophers. This "why and how" point has to be recognized and resolved in all scientific pursuits, but in every area it has to be relearned as if it had never been faced before. Luria has worked for years on speech and language based on aphasia (the loss of speech, usually due to brain damage). His work has had to do with areas of the brain related to speech, and the identification of the components of speech through this approach, and the rebuilding of the speech process once it is lost. His studies have been precise and detailed (micro) to the point that a less persistent person would be driven to distraction. Vygotsky and Luria were engaged in what is now called the study of cognitive processes long before the western world gave it any serious thought. One view of cognitive psychology might be: "the study of the relation of language to thought and the acquisition of knowledge (Luria, 1981)."

Cognitive Psychology Supports the Language Mode. The above discussions (concerning the writings of Bruner, Neisser, Hart, Vygotsky, and Luria) have been for the purpose of establishing the relationship of language and its development, to thought, cognitive processes, and the acquisition of knowledge. All this is necessary to understand and appreciate why the new teaching method in the basic literacy dimension of the school curriculum is in the "language mode."

American Scholarship Supports Vygotsky. The recent publication, *Advances in Child Development and Behavior*, Volume 16 (1982), reviews research in six areas of child development, the first of which is "Social Bases of Language Development: A Reassessment (Bates, 1982)." This review recognizes the importance of Vygotsky's work by structuring much of the review around his three major lines of research (Vygotsky, 1962): "(1) correlations between attachment and language, (2) studies of preverbal interaction between child and caretaker, and (3) studies of motherese." Vygotsky "stressed the powerful *social motivation* of the infant to imitate and interact with other human beings as she or he sees it . . . Gradually, linguistic structure begins to accompany the child's own private interactions with the world—talking out loud to oneself in play, using language to announce, "guide," and anticipate actions to come and to note the results of actions that have been completed. Through this process of *accompaniment*, language gradually takes on a *governing* role, structuring and directing tool thought. This governing role becomes more rapid and efficient, "talking aloud" in turn, becomes abbreviated, the language moves "inside" to become the master of thought from there on (Bates, 1982)." This is what Vygotsky means by "thought becomes socialized;" the basic values of our culture are embodied in the language, language is the means of interaction with the culture, and since language becomes the master of thought, thought becomes socialized. This comes very close to being a correlary to the writer's summary of the new theory: "motivation to learn is a social phenomenon."

Support for Direct Instruction. In November, 1975 a group of psychologists, educators, and philosophers met on Shelter Island in the San Diego harbor to reflect on schooling and the acquisition of knowledge. This study group was sponsored by the Navy Personnel Research and Development Center. The preface to the book published as a result of that conference points to the great change that has occurred in the field of psychology in the last fifteen years. The switch to an emphasis on cognitive psychology is described as a major revolution in that field of study. Quoting the preface directly:

> During the past decade and a half there has been a ferment in psychology. . . . The whole point of view about what constitutes the proper goal of psychology has changed. . . . Nontheless, at the present time, work in cognitive psychology and related fields has had only modest impact on the thinking of educational researchers, and virtually no disciplined application to instructional practice. . . . The one common thread running through all of the formal papers and dialogue was that the knowledge a person already possesses is the principal determiner of what that individual can learn from an educational experience (Anderson, 1977).

Chapter Eleven of this book is a review of literature titled, "The Acquisition of Knowledge in the Classroom (Berliner and Rosenshine, 1977)." After reviewing research on curriculum, method, teaching aids, etc., and concluding that research in these areas has been inconclusive, the writers turn to analysis of the data based on whether it supports active, direct instruction by the teacher using classroom size groups. Defining direct instruction they write:

> Direct instruction means a set of teaching behaviors that focus on academic matters in which goals are clear to students, time allocated for instruction is sufficient and continuous, content coverage is extensive, student performance is monitored, questions are at a low cognitive level producing

many correct responses, and feedback to students is immediate and academically oriented. The teacher controls instructional goals, choosing material appropriate for the student's ability level, and pacing the instructional episode. Interaction is characterized as structured but not authoritarian. Rather, learning takes place in a convivial academic atmosphere (Berliner and Rosenshine, 1977).

After giving the research support for each component in the above paragraph, Berliner and Rosenshine conclude with:

That is, almost all teacher behaviors that increase a classes engagement with the content of almost any curriculum, communicated to students through almost any teaching method, will increase student achievement (Berliner and Rosenshine, 1977).

It is interesting to note a qualification concerning academic and non-academic feedback:

It appears that feedback to students, whether praise or criticism, helps students acquire knowledge, providing the feedback is academically focused. This is a major determinant of student achievement (Berliner and Rosenshine, 1977).

This observation is consistent with Hofstede's thesis concerning the administration of international corporations: that people of different cultures can profitably work together on the expressed goals of the corporation (Hofstede, 1980).

Add Frank Smith and We Have a New Theory of Learning. The information given by Frank Smith concerning "What the Eye Tells the Brain" (Chapter 7 of his book: *Understanding Reading*) is so important to the curriculum organization and teaching method in the school built on the new theory that an extensive quotation and paraphrase is given from his discussion of the restrictions placed on the reading process by the existence of the short-term memory:

The fact that the eye is open and exposed to stimulation by light is no indication that visual information is being received and processed by the brain. The eye is exposed to much more information than the brain can possibly use, and the brain selects and processes only as much as it can handle. And while the brain is busy constructing one percept the system appears to be closed to new information that might be arriving from the eyes. Yet just as we see no spatial discontinuity at the point where the separate visual experiences from the two halves of our field of view are brought together, so we are unaware of the discontinuity over time that occurs with a visual system that is in effect "taking snapshots" of the world no faster than four times a second (Smith, 1971).

Dr. Smith goes on to describe the tachistoscope; an instrument made for flashing images from slides to a screen for measured periods of time. With this instrument psychologists have determined that the eye needs only $\frac{1}{20}$ of a second or less to register all the information it can receive in a single fixation. If the time is extended to $\frac{1}{4}$ second, the individual will report no additional information (Smith and Carey, 1966). In spite of the very short time needed for a single fixation, the eye can do this operation no faster than four times a second. (Review: the eye needs $\frac{1}{20}$ second or less to record a single clump of information, yet it can record only four clumps of information per second. So in a period of one second it is "seeing" only one-fifth of the time, leaving four-fifths of a second to space. What is going on in this extra time?)

The next major finding from the tachistoscope is that the amount of information that can be received in the $\frac{1}{20}$ of a second depends on the previous learning of the viewer. If random letters are shown, the viewer reports only four or five, if random words are shown, the viewer reports only four or five, if random phrases are shown, the viewer reports only four or five. This is true only if the viewer is familiar with the letters, words, or phrases (Cattell, 1947).

Dr. Smith points out that the real significance of these tachistocopic studies was ignored because it led to the great controversy concerning "word or letter" method for teaching reading. It took sixty years from the time it was discovered that only four or five items could be "seen" in a single eye fixation before it was discovered that this was not a limitation of the eye in seeing "but rather by a log jam in the processing" of that information.

Dr. Smith reports that a series of experiments dealing with "partial recall" identifies this log jam is the result of the limited capacity of the short-term memory. A typical experiment is as follows: The subject is told that he/she will be shown in a fraction of a second a pattern of 12 random letters displayed in three lines and four columns. The subject is also told that at the time the display is shown, a high, middle, or low tone will be sounded. If a high tone is sounded, the subject is to report the top line; if a middle tone is sounded, the middle line is reported; and if a low tone, the bottom line.

When the experiment is carried out, the subject reads the four letters without difficulty. Then after reading one line, as called for by the tone, the subject is asked to recall a second line of the three. This the subject cannot do. But the subject sees nothing strange in this. The key to the experiment is: *The subject was not told that the tone sounded after the visual image left the screen.* If the subject could read any line of the three, but was not "told" which line to read until the picture was gone from the screen, it means that the subject had to remember the three lines (and the 12 letters) until the tone was sounded. Then, if the subject could not report but one line, it means that the reporting (or processing) of that single line of four letters interferes with the memory of the other two lines (8 letters). This Dr. Smith identifies with a phenomenon called "masking." It requires approximately five seconds to process a single visual display to the long-term memory. If something intervenes within that time, the short-term memory fades away. To retain information long enough to be stored in the long-term memory, time must be left for rehearsal of the information (Smith 1971).

The New Theory of Learning. Language acquisition has been tied to social interaction, and exposed as being willful and purposeful. Language moves from being an accompaniment of action to a governing role, structuring and controlling thought. The brain is not a passive instrument. It not only chooses what it will react to, it chooses what it will observe. It is not the slave of its environment; it structures the environment to its liking. Its tool of thought is the word and language. The greatest restrictor on thought is the lack of a word. If the brain has half-a-chance, it relates ideas and words without conscious effort by the person. The teacher's duty is to expose the brain to language (knowledge in language form). This from the cognitive psychologists. Add the Frank Smith analysis of the short-term memory and we have a new theory of learning or a new theory of knowledge acquisition.

If words are the tools of thought, and the short-term memory consists of a funnel through which only four or five items can pass at a time, blocking other items in the process; and if these items consist of word-like symbols representing semantic fields (meanings) then; *the learning process must consist of the expansion of the meaning attached to the symbols* and not a building process consisting of adding micro blocks to the brain storage.

1492 might be four numerals occupying the full capacity of the short-term memory. It might be recognized as a single date and become one unit of four items being processed through the short-term memory. Or it might expand to Columbus, and the discovery of America. Or it might represent, to a student of history, the whole historical period of new world discovery. Or it may in one word represent a life's work of a scholar.

It is interesting to note that while the short-term memory is restricted to 3, 4 or 5 items in one short period of time and that the processing of these items blocks out (called "masking") other items while these 3, 4 or 5 are being processed—it seems that there is no restriction placed on the *size* of the items involved. It is required that each item be so familiar to the learner that the items themselves do not have to be examined, thought about, or reconstructed at the time it is processed through the short-term memory. This suggests that the process of learning is quite different from that implied in the widely accepted micro-stepped, sequential curriculum. In this context *the process of learning is perceived as closely paralleling that of learning a language.* There is no necessary beginning point, there is no necessary sequence, there is no progression from simple to complex, nor from concrete to abstract. (These ideas are useful to the researcher, but they furnish little direction and no security to the teacher and the curriculum builder.) The learner is introduced to words and other signs and symbols that designate objects, actions, properties, or relationships. The relationship between the word and its meaning is very complex. The meaning expands, is modified, expands again, is reconstructed from scratch, old meanings dropped, and new meanings adopted. As symbols and expanded meanings become quite familiar (not requiring synthesis in order to use); the expanded unit can then be fed through the short-term memory without hesitation. This suggests that the basic languages must be learned well and that we avoid as long as possible saying that the process of learning is knowing where to find it. Knowing where to find it is a refinement to the scheme and not its essence.

In Language Development Writing is the Basic Activity. The analysis Dr. Frank Smith makes of the short-term memory research gives a logic to the power of writing in the thinking process. As the thinker writes, the written words serve to hold ideas in place ready to be processed through the memory slot, relieving the thought mechanisms of holding on to words for future processing. Writers for years have contended that putting an idea on paper stimulates additional thought about it.

In a system of listening, speaking, reading, and writing; writing is paramount. It is the only one that requires the other three. Writing, like speaking, is active while listening and reading are passive. Listeners and readers are users of the system;

speakers and writers are producers of the system. Speaking is transitory while writing is permanent.

Dr. Kenneth Levine, the noted British sociologist, whose major professional interest is literacy, makes a much stronger statement favoring writing related to specific knowledge as the most important component of literacy. In the initial article of the Harvard Educational Review of August 1982 Dr. Levine challenges the existing notion of "functional literacy" and concludes in the last sentence:

> The social and political significance of literacy is very largely derived from its role in creating and reproducing - or failing to reproduce - the social distribution of knowledge. If this were not so, if literacy did not have this role, the inability to read would be a shortcoming on a par with tone-deafness, while an ability to write would be as socially inconsequential as a facility for whistling a tune (Levine, 1982).

Chapter 9

Summary

There was a definite Aha! phenomenon in the fall of 1971. This took place after three or four class sessions in which the writer was teaching a class called "Theories of Educational Administration." The materials on which the class was based were inherited from a previous "theory" professor. The writer realized that there was no theory - that the materials reflected only a "search for" theory. The Aha! came directly from the realization that most of the books on the subject began with Max Weber. The Aha! was that there *is a theory*! Unspoken, unrecognized, but real: the Max Weber bureaucratic model, the production model, the factory model. The major attempt to improve education since Sputnik (1957) all fit the production model.

The production model solution was a natural decision, made, unconsciously, under extreme political and social pressure. Sputnik produced the pressure, and Sputnik produced the answer. The USSR put a small silver ball into space orbit. The U.S. answers by putting a man on the moon. Education simply followed the "man on the moon" syndrome. We, in effect, said, "Any people that can put a man on the moon can surely. . ." solve the problem of producing superior education for children and youth, in an "everybody-in-school" education system, in a free and democratic society. We decided the answer was simple: follow the plan that put us on the moon! And we moved quickly into the process of refining the production model.

The writer was offered the directorship of a research and development center that operated on a federal, annual budget of $800,000. Knowing unofficially that the center was scheduled for closing in two years (1970), he went to Washington to assess the possibility of saving the center. He was told that it would be necessary to produce a sound theoretical base for the operation. Returning to the center, he asked a former official of the center to state the theoretical basis for the operation. Answer: "Gene, you know damn well, if you start sooner and teach harder the kids will learn more." A clean, simple, uncomplicated statement of the production model!

But it's not a theory; it's technology, which to work, presupposes sound theory. The theories that put the man on the moon were not, PERT, nor PPBS, nor MBO (you can't get to the moon if you don't first know where you are going.) The theories that put the man on the moon are the precise descriptions of nature that have been forged by scientists since 1600. It didn't begin with Einstein's $E = MC^2$ but Galileo's $v = kt$ which led directly to $s = \frac{1}{2}kt^2$.

Then the research on new efforts to improve on education began to come out. The writer first made his own summaries, because the usual commentaries were strongly resisting and rebutting the evidence (the new stuff no better, no worse than the old). A short time later came the first clear, authoritative statement, by reputable evaluators of research. The "Rand Report" (1972) stated as Proposition 1: "Research has not identified a variant of the existing system that is consistently related to student's educational outcomes."

The neutral results of research were interpreted by the writer as a direct challenge of the production model. But, as said before, the production model is technology, not theory. There is an unrecognized theoretical base for the production model, but what is it? At this point we go back to the concept of basic theory and *Describe the school*! The Galileo breakthrough was when he decided to *describe* the free falling body, and stop the useless pursuit of "why does it fall?"

The writer found an answer through the examination of his African experience while trying to help introduce American type education into developing countries (Ethiopia, 1965–67; Nigeria, 1970–71). The American type school, as presented to the developing countries, is the comprehensive school, often called over there, "the modern school." This the education leaders intellectually reject, because they know that the United States has not solved the problem of universal education in a free democratic society. They feel that they must cooperate in trying to establish the American type "modern school," because they consider it an absolute political necessity. The only alternative, as they see it, is the clearly understood universal education of the communist state.

The writer saw that the problem was generated by the expansion of a school system that was still basically the old colonial school or the missionary school, into a system of education for all. He decided that this was impossible as an add-on process, and he saw that adding the comprehensive idea to the missionary-colonial school only caused the serious students to escape the school, if this were possible, leaving the public schools to the poor and disadvantaged.

He then defined a missionary-colonial school (now called TYPE TWO) as being a school where the students' motivation to learn is based on the desire of the individual student to acquire something the school had to offer. Putting all children or youth in this school destroys this motivational system.

This, by contrast, identified the system of education designed "for everybody" as the education system of the closed society: the village. So the writer defined a second kind of school: that school that is produced by a closed social system in which the students' motivation is that furnished by the total social environment of the village of which the education system is a part (then called Village-Tribal; now called the TYPE ONE SCHOOL). It is obvious that such a system cannot be effective from a poly-cultural base. This TYPE ONE and TYPE TWO describes a social model that says rather strongly that motivation to learn is a social phenomenon. This two-dimensional model also furnishes a theoretical basis for the technical system called the "production model," because it says that if you cannot claim that the individual student brings his own individual motivation to school (which you cannot claim if everybody is in school), and you cannot claim that the students' motivation is the value system of a monolithic culture (which you cannot claim if the school has a poly-cultural base), then you are forced to conclude that when you have all in school in a poly-cultural society, the means of production (identified now as a social phenomenon) must be "within" the school.

It may seem on the surface that we have reasoned in a circle, starting with the production model and ending with the production model. However, in the process we have done two things: (1) we have "explained" why (produced a theoretical basis for) attempts to improve education in a poly-cultural society, where every child and youth is expected to be in school, we *must* assume the production model; and (2) we have produced the theoretical basis for what must be the organization, the curriculum, and the teaching method in the school which assumes that the motivational basis for learning must be produced at school. It is clear that the school must work at some kind of social approach in developing motivation to learn what the school teaches. This defines THE TYPE THREE SCHOOL.

Now we return to the research findings concerning attempts to improve education since Sputnik (1957). We have noted that the research results are essentially neutral. A second consistent finding is that the major factors correlated to measured student achievement are largely outside the school.

When we apply the idea generated by the new theory to the research data, we discover that the outside-the-school factors are also social/societal/cultural in nature; confirming the deduction from the new theory that motivation to learn is a social phenomenon.

We now have firm direction for what must go on inside the school. The efforts to achieve maximum learning in a school that has a poly-cultural base and a school in which all children and youth are presumed to be in school, must stem from a social base.

The writer has interpreted this to mean that a school culture must be produced within the school and that this is achieved by the building and maintaining strong student groups.

From this point on, the major decision for the writer was whether to use the theory to make minimum corrections to the present system of schooling, or to pursue the theory as purely as possible without regard to what now exists. The decision was for the latter, because such an approach more clearly defines the theory and all its implications.

Having made this decision, the writer proceeded to propose school practices that build and support the group processes while eliminating present school practice that is not supported by the theory.

John Tyndall (1820–1893) in eulogizing the great Michael Faraday (1791–1867) made a statement concerning theory and the use of theory that has become a classic:

> In our conceptions and reasonings regarding the forces of nature, we perpetually make use of symbols which, when they possess a high representative value, we dignify with the name of theories. Thus, prompted by certain analogies we ascribe electrical phenomena to the action of a peculiar fluid, sometimes flowing, sometimes at rest. Such conceptions have their advantages and their disadvantages; they afford peaceful lodging to the intellect for a time, but they also circumscribe it, and by and by, when the mind has grown too large for its lodging, it often finds difficulty in breaking down the walls of what has become its prison instead of its home.
>
> (John Tyndall, Faraday as a discoverer, London, 1877, new ed.)

Chapter 10

A Final Word

I have called this book "The Coming Revolution in Education" because: first, I believe that educational practice has been worked into a corner from which it cannot gracefully extricate itself. If it gets out, it will have to break out, not ooze out. The breakout, if it happens, will produce great trauma in more areas than is commonly recognized as educational. For example, the publishing and printing industries are so deeply involved in public school education that it is unclear how much of educational practice is actually controlled by that group. The complexities of the involvement of education in all segments of the economic and business world is enough to produce great resistance to fundamental change, just from fear of the unknown or unpredictable results.

Second, major change in education in the past has not come from ideas advanced by educational thinkers. There is usually an idea involved in great change, but the power behind the movement is always economic and social. Great wars change everything. The big result of World War I was communist Russia; the big result of World War II was communist China.

I have two purposes in presenting this book: first, the theory furnishes a basis for understanding the problems and frustrations that face all involved in the education process who are trying to live up to the social and political mandate of "everybody in school." Second, I wish to put the theory into the public record, anticipating the time when social and political conditions may make great change in education possible.

The growing discontent by the public with the work of the education establishment will not, in itself, produce major change. The prevalence of fast and universal communication systems and devices makes it possible for educators to stay a step ahead (or a step behind) the public in its discontent. The prime competence of the institution of public education, that has progressed to the point that its main purpose is survival, is the ability to devise short-term answers to the short-term concerns of the public (the political public seldom exhibits long-term concerns).

While it is probably true that major change in education will have to await the arrival of a major social or economic crisis, I believe there are two identifiable trends that are not likely to be reversed.

One: There is a steady and strong trend toward a federal medical and health program for all Americans. As long as such a program was perceived as free medical care for the poor, it was subject to the periodic swings from conservative to liberal and back. The cost of medical care, the growing cost of technical medical equipment, and a growing reluctance by the public to deny any expensive treatment to anyone on humanitarian grounds regardless of ability to pay, seems to lead to some kind of federally sponsored program. I believe that the next major move in that direction will be a complete medical and health service for children and youth. Public education should be ready with a program that makes the combining of schooling and health services a natural progression. Combining education and health services would form a reasonable basis for the solution to the persistent problem of a logical division of federal and state responsibility for education. The medical service would be federal—the rest of the program would be financed by state and local taxation.

Two: The movement of women into the job market will not be reversed. Any conceivable crisis would increase the pace of this movement rather than decrease it. "The single most outstanding phenomenon of our century is the huge number of women who are entering the labor force. Its long-term implications are absolutely unchartable." Eli Ginzberg (Briggs - 1977).

This statement was made by Eli Ginzberg in an interview with a writer of Forbes Magazine in 1977. Dr. Ginzberg is a Columbia University economist and a well-known specialist on human resources. He was chairman of the National Commission on Manpower Policy, and advisor on manpower to many U.S. presidents. If we assume that we are moving into a social condition in which all adults are presumed to be employed, the public schools should be prepared to accept the responsibility of providing a safe, wholesome, healthy, disciplined place for children and youth while parents work. Good school practice would require that such a program be combined with other normal school functions, and not be considered an added chore.

If the two conditions do materialize (health and medical service for youth and a setting where all adults are expected to work), the school based on the new theory would be appropriate (Boyce, 1981). If the crisis required for major change came about without the two above conditions, the proposed new school could not materialize.

I would not advise the attempted adoption of the new school if the planners perceive, or work on the assumption that they are dealing with a monolithic culture. Under the new theory it would be assumed that there would be no major problems in such an education system (This would automatically produce a TYPE ONE or Village-Tribal school).

I would not advise the attempted adoption of the new school if the planners have no real concern for those who do not wish to cooperate in their own education, or if the planners do not fear the political consequences generated by a large number of citizens untrained for life in a scientifically based technical society (This point-of-view produces the TYPE TWO or the Missionary-Colonial School). The strong "back-to-basics" movement is of this type, accepting the drop-out as a normal consequence of a strong education system.

Purposely avoided in this book has been the extension of the details of the curriculum and teaching method into the early school and the secondary school, not because it is unimportant, nor because it can be permanently avoided, but because I felt this would be quite tedious in a short book and would at least double the space required for the theory statement.

Avoided also, is the powerful support given the theory from the history of theory development in the physical sciences, an interest of mine for many years. The theory clearly was triggered by the two experiences in Africa, but I have a strong suspicion that the theory would not have bloomed as an Aha! phenomenon, had not the physical science theory semantic field existed in my mind. This approach to the new theory requires more knowledge of mathematics and physical science than the average educator possesses. I do, however, tackle this problem in the third of three graduate courses based on the new theory. I am planning a second publication that uses this physical science approach. Mathematicians would call this a more powerful argument than the one presented in this book.

Finally, I return to the concluding statement of my original theory paper written in 1976. "The day may come when citizens in a comparatively free society can entertain the notion that complete freedom for the youth may not be the best preparation for a life in a free society, and that schools in such a system may need to give as much attention to the power of peer approval and support as do schools in managed social systems (Boyce, 1976)."

References

Anderson, R. C., Spiro, R. J., & Montague, W. E. (Ed.) *Schooling and the acquisition of knowledge.* Hillsdale, N.J.: Lawrence Erlbaum Assoc., 1977.

Averich, Harvey A., et. al. *How effective is schooling? A critical review and synthesis of research findings.* Santa Monica: Rand Corporation, March 1972.

Bates, Elizabeth et. al. Social bases of language development: a reassessment. *Advances in Child Development and Behavior,* Vol. 16. New York: Academic Press, 1982.

Berliner, David C. and Rosenshine, Barak. The acquisition of knowledge in the classroom. Chapter 11 of R.C. Anderson, R.I. Spiro, and Montague, *Schooling and the Acquisition of Knowledge.* Hillsdale, N.J.: Lawrence Erlbaum Assoc., Publishers, 1977.

Berman, Paul, et. al. *Federal Programs Supporting Educational Change.* Santa Monica: Rand Corporation, R–1589/4 - HEW, April 1975.

Boyce, E. M. We need a handbook . . . In R. C. Pucinski (Chairman), *Needs of Elementary and Secondary Education for the Seventies: A Compendium of Policy Papers.* General Committee on Education of the Committee on Education and Labor, House of Representatives, Ninety-First Congress. U.S. Government Printing House, March 1970, pp. 50–53.

Boyce, E. M. A basic theory for educators. *Conference on the Public and Public Education.* Atlanta, Georgia: Committee for the Humanities in Georgia, Sept. 1976.

Boyce, E. M. The institutionalized middle school. *American Middle School Education.* Athens, Ga., Spring, 1978.

Boyce, E. M. *The future in education: rewind or fast forward.* A paper published for a television series by the Tri-County Regional Library, Rome, Georgia. Sponsored by the National Endowment for the Humanities. Rome, Georgia, 1981.

Briggs, Jean A. How you going to get 'em back in the kitchen? (You aren't.) *Forbes,* November 15, 1977, 177–184.

Bronfenbrenner, U. *Two kinds of childhood: U.S. and U.S.S.R.* New York: Russel Sage Foundation, 1970.

Brown, C. L. Socio-economic background and achievement in the middle school. *Middle School Journal,* 1978, 9(1), 5.

Bruner, Jerome S. *The process of education.* Cambridge: University Press, 1960.

Bruner, Jerome S. Culture, politics, and pedagogy. *Saturday Review,* May 18, 1968, 69–72, 89–90.

Bruner, Jerome S. Understanding psychological man: a state of the science report. *Psychology Today,* May 1982, 40–43.

Cattell, J. M. *Man of science, 1860–1944.* Lancaster, PA: Science Press, 1947.

Curran, Edward A. NIE: an agenda for the 80's. *Educational Researcher,* May 1982, 11(5), 10–21.

Goodlad, John I. What goes on in our schools? *Educational Researcher,* March 1977, 3, 3–6.

Goodlad, John I., Sirotnik, Kenneth A., & Overman, Betty C. An overview of "a study of schooling." *Phi Delta Kappan,* November 1979, 61(3), 174–178.

Gross, N. Theoretical and policy implications of case study findings about federal efforts to improve public schools. *Annals AAPSS,* 1977, 434, 71–87.

Gross, N. and Herriott, R. *The dynamics of planned educational change*. Berkeley, Calif.: McCutchan, 1979.

Hart, Leslie A. The new brain concept of learning. *Phi Delta Kappan*, February 1978, *59*(6), 393–396.

Hipple, Theodore W. (Ed.). *The future of education: 1975–2000*. Pacific Palisades: Goodyear Publishing Company, 1975.

Hofstede, Geert. *Cultures consequences: international differences in work related values*. Cross Cultural Research and Methodological Series, No. 5. Beverly Hills: Sage Publications, 1980.

Kessen, William. Questions for a theory of cognitive development in concept development. *Monographs of the Society for Research in Child Development*, 1966, *31*(No. 5).

Levine, Kenneth. Functional literacy: fond illusions and false economics. *Harvard Educational Review*, 1982, *52*, 249–266.

Luria, Alexander R. *Language and cognition*. Washington, D.C.: H. V. Winston and Sons, 1981.

Neisser, Ulric. Understanding psychological man: the state of the science. *Psychology Today*, May, 1982, 44–48.

Phillips, D. C., & Kelly, Mavis E. Hierarchical theories of development in education and psychology. *Harvard Educational Review*, August 1975, *45*(3), 351–375.

Pucinski, Roman C. *Needs of elementary and secondary education for the seventies*. (Compiled by the General Subcommittee on Education of the Committee on Education and Labor, House of Representatives, Ninety-first Congress.) Washington, D.C.: U.S. Government Printing Office, March 1970.

Sanders, Donald P. Educational inquiry as developmental research. *Educational Researcher*, March 1981, *10*(3), 8–13.

Smith, Frank and Cary P. Temporal factors in visual information processing. *Canadian Journal of Psychology*, 1966, *20*(3), 337–342.

Smith, Frank. *Understanding reading: a psycholinguistic analysis of reading and learning to read.* New York: Holt, Rinehart and Winston, 1971.

Suppes, P. The place of theory in educational research. *Educational Researcher*, 1974, *3*(6), 3–10.

Vygotsky, L. S. *Thought and language*, Cambridge, Mass.: MIT Press, 1962.

EUGENE M. BOYCE
is a Professor of Education of Administration in the College of Education at the University of Georgia. He has spent his entire life in education administration from the position of high school principal to the position of Educational Advisor in—at different times—Ethiopia and Nigeria. It was in Africa that the seeds of his educational theory were planted. There he realized that America has not solved the problem of universal education in a free democratic society. Educational practice has worked itself into a corner. If it gets out, it will have to break out. Only great changes in social and political conditions will make a great change in education possible. Revolution.

Randall Library – UNCW

LC1035 .B69 1983

NXWW

Boyce / The coming revolution in education : basic

3049002868401